TOTAL QUALITY MANAGEMENT

Breaking down the barriers

Nick Develin
Max Hand
Develin & Partners

Accountancy BOOKS
IN BUSINESS

The Institute of Chartered Accountants
in England and Wales
Chartered Accountants' Hall
Moorgate Place
London EC2P 2BJ

British Library Cataloguing-in-Publication Data.
A catalogue record for this book is available from the British Library.

Typeset by Type Study, Scarborough, North Yorkshire.
Printed in Great Britain by Hartnolls, Bodmin, Cornwall

Contents

Foreword

How many places of work do you know where, the moment the boss's back is turned, the people there say: You would not believe what goes on here? And they then recite a catalogue of misery.

Nobody knows what anybody else is up to. Nothing goes smoothly. There is only delay, confusion, error, waste and unnecessary cost.

That, I submit, is the absence of quality management.

How many places of work do you know where everyone knows what everyone else is up to? Everything goes smoothly. There is no hanging about waiting for this or that to happen.

Everything which has to happen is looked at as a whole. Everything and everyone.

That, I believe, is Total Quality management.

Nick Develin and Max Hand know that to achieve Total Quality companies have to discard the habits of a lifetime.

But they also know that it is not enough for managements to be mesmerised by the incantations of consultants and to walk about chanting absolutes. That way they disappear up their own vocabularies.

Nor is it enough for a workforce to dismiss theory and insist that it is all a matter of common sense. If it were, we would all be doing it.

The pursuit of quality requires the application of intelligence to the business activity by everyone to everything.

The first thing a company needs is a very clear idea of what it is about in the whole process from instructing the supplier to supplying the customer.

The thinking and the methods and the means must be applied to the total business, otherwise problems simply mount up elsewhere.

It is no use increasing production and productivity on the factory floor if the goods are piling up in the warehouse. There must be quality at every stage.

There must be no more excuses. No more saying: Oh that will do, that will get by. No way.

Near enough is not good enough. The Japanese have a phrase for it: zero defects. But even that is slightly negative. Better: everything right first time. Spot on.

And that is achieved not by telling people what to do, ordering them about, but by telling them what is required, knowing that they have been given the training and have the skills to know what to do.

The reason for pursuing Total Quality is not because it is more efficient (though it is), and not because it is more profitable (though it must be), but because it makes people happy.

Nothing is more demoralising than working in a shambles. To make a better job of work requires making a better use of people. And the reward is not only shared prosperity but real job satisfaction.

That is Total Quality at work.

Brian Redhead

Preface

Many books have been written about Total Quality. Anyone setting out to write another one must believe that they have something new to say. If the approach to management that Total Quality represents were merely sterile theory, or a prescription to cure the ills of commercial life, there would be little more to add. We believe there is more to say.

The principles that underpin Total Quality represent a universal morality that is common to any civilised culture, and that is relevant to any decent human endeavour: pleasing others, improving, self-fulfilment, respect, enjoyment.

One of our colleagues was once asked to outline the 'intellectual, research-based, philosophical basis' for our approach to total quality. He replied: 'to have a nice day'. Nobody should have to go to work to carry out wasteful and soul-destroying tasks. Nobody should be demeaned by the system they are part of. Nobody should be a victim. Enterprise is profitable only when it delivers value for money, and value can only be created by people.

We sometimes forget the meaning of the word 'company' – people who cooperate with each other to deliver products and services to others. Any approach to management, including Total Quality, therefore concerns how to get people to cooperate so as to add value.

We believe we have something to say about the barriers to creating value, about the behaviour that causes them, and about how to break them down.

Nick Develin
Max Hand

Develin & Partners
211 Piccadilly
London W1V 9LE

CHAPTER 1

Introduction

'. . . bump, bump, bump, on the back of his head, behind Christopher Robin. It is, as far as he knows, the only way to come downstairs, but sometimes he feels that there really is another way, if only he could stop bumping for a moment and think of it.'

A.A. Milne

Dr W. Edwards Deming, one of the principal gurus of Total Quality Management, claims that by the end of the century, there will be only two types of business. Those that practice Total Quality, and those that are no longer in business.

If this is an exaggeration, it is not much of one. The truth of the message is emphasised by the success of the Japanese and lately by newly industrialised countries such as Taiwan and Singapore. World competition has been intensified by the effectiveness of the management style adopted by successful companies in such countries. Our own economy is changing rapidly as industry after industry is restructured and reshaped to try to keep up with the competition. Too many UK industries have failed and been lost to competition abroad – motor cycles, cars, textiles, consumer electronics and shipbuilding to name a few – to make complacency acceptable.

To survive in the future, we must not only learn from those companies that now set the standard for global competition: we must also build on our own strengths and culture to match and overtake them. This is management's job. We must learn new ways of running companies. This does not mean 'becoming like the Japanese' or anyone else.

There is a common belief that Total Quality is something peculiar to the Japanese or Eastern culture, and that it sits uncomfortably in our Western – or particularly British – culture. There is nothing ethnic about putting the customer first, about striving to do things right first time, or about taking the

1

long-term view. Nor is it contrary to Western culture to respect individual capabilities, to empower staff, to enable people to take pride in their work, and to encourage team work.

The principles described in this book have been practised by those leading Japanese companies that have so successfully assaulted Western companies over the last 30 years. In the West, we are only just beginning to understand them and put them into practice.

The task is urgent. And yet, Total Quality is not widely practised or understood. It is not new, nor did it start in Japan. Its origins can be traced back almost 70 years to the first use of statistical tools to improve the quality of manufactured products in the United States.

After the Second World War, the USA turned its attention to meeting an insatiable demand for consumer products. For almost 15 years, there was only token foreign competition. In a period of unparalleled prosperity and growth, poor, costly and inefficient management practices passed unnoticed.

Japan, a nation lacking in natural resources, needed to export in order to feed its people. In the 1950s, American gurus including Deming and Juran received a ready response to their message of quality improvement from top Japanese management. Throughout the 1960s the quality gap between Japan and the West narrowed. By the early 1970s the gap had been transposed. Japanese products, in the 1960s justifiably termed little better than 'junk', were setting a standard of quality that many western companies could not even begin to compete with.

Western managers have been slow to respond. It was only in the early 1980s that companies began the Total Quality journey, almost three decades after the first Japanese companies took their first steps down the same road. We are only now realising that our lack of competitiveness is not just the result of Japanese success: it is also the result of our own failure to manage.

Can we ever catch up? The signs are uncertain. Recent surveys[1] have found that as many as 80 per cent of companies that have embarked on Total Quality have been disappointed by the results. Equally, a small but growing number of American, European and British companies have demonstrated astonishing achievements through the application of the principles of Total Quality: Motorola, British Airways, ICL, Rank Xerox to name a few.

What is quality?

Someone once remarked that 'quality is like obscenity. It's hard to define, but you know it when you see it'.

Put simply, quality means meeting customer requirements. Quality has to be defined from the customers' perspective. Their requirements may include availability, reliability, design, delivery, and many other features.

Some years ago, when Ford first understood the extent of Japan's lead in the automotive industry, the company embarked on a change programme dubbed 'AJ' (After Japan), in a bid to eliminate the competitive advantage that its Japanese competitors had gained. One exercise involved studying the quality of radiators manufactured by Toyota. An engineer was sent to buy four Toyota radiators to be dismantled for examination by Ford's production engineers. He reported back that they could not be purchased as spare parts, because they were only supplied direct from a central warehouse in the UK to accident repairers. It came as something of a shock to Ford to be told that if the radiators were still wanted as replacement parts, they would be delivered by air from Japan, but that they would be accompanied by a team of engineers *whose job it would be to find out why the radiators had failed in normal service.*

Over the years, our thinking on the definition of quality has changed greatly. In Philip Crosby's earlier books,[2] he described quality as 'meeting the specification'. This description implies that between two limits of tolerance, quality is good, but anything outside those limits is not. This gave rise to the notion of 'Zero Defects'. Deming was one of those who objected to this definition, on the grounds that it discouraged continuous improvement.

Since then, the customer has played an increasingly important role in determining how we think about quality.

Companies are responding by trying to go beyond the customer's expectations – delivering that little bit more than their competitors to make their products or service distinctive.

What is Total Quality?

Total Quality is a system of behaviour which embraces everyone within an organisation and which determines their relationships with the outside world – customers, suppliers, competitors, society and the environment. Its driving principle is continuous improvement.

Any system of behaviour must have shared beliefs and values, and a common purpose. Everyone must be committed to these, *and act accordingly.*

In describing Total Quality as a system of behaviour, we distinguish between the end results and the means of achieving them. The end results might be continuously improving levels of product and service quality, delivered at continuously reducing cost, providing increasing levels of customer satisfaction, which together lead to greater profitability. The issue is how such results are achieved: people throughout the business have to interact and cooperate in order to meet the customers' needs.

We distinguish, too, between attitudes and behaviour. It is striking that in many organisations, individuals can hold convictions entirely in line with the tenets of Total Quality – such as putting the customer first, cooperating across functional boundaries, and empowering staff – *yet behave in a way that is demonstrably at variance with those beliefs*. Why does this happen?

Certainly, people do not usually do it consciously. When it happens, the result is invariably frustration and low morale.

> *A bank established a centralised unit to provide branches with foreign currency and travellers' cheques. In line with the bank's customer care programme, the unit established methods and processes to provide a responsive and proactive service to branches (anticipating demand at branch level during the holiday season, managing distribution economically using the bank's bullion runs, and so forth). Inexplicably, demand from the branches fell, and it transpired that branches were buying currency and cheques from competitors! The reason was simple: every branch and central unit in the bank was treated as a profit centre and required to make a 'contribution'. The Treasury function charged the unit for the currency it 'bought', plus a margin; and the transport function charged the unit for distribution, plus a margin. The unit likewise charged branches, plus a margin. Unsurprisingly, the branches found competitors' prices cheaper, and bought from them in order to keep their own costs down, even though they took longer to supply. The accounts department spent a lot of time managing all the cross-charges and trying unsuccessfully to reconcile departmental contributions with overall profit.*

Clearly, the result was in the best interests of neither the bank nor its customers. In this case, departmental 'contribution to profit' was the dominant driver of behaviour. Branch managers knew that whatever management *said* about the importance of customer service, their own and their branch's performance would be judged by the contribution figure.

The point of this story is that nobody perceived any inconsistency between using contribution as a measure of performance, and exhortation to improve customer service. The branches simply regarded the currency unit's high prices as a typical example of head office incompetence. The currency unit saw branches as a law unto themselves. Both *believed* in customer service, but their *behaviour* contradicted that belief, and the resulting frustration was easily blamed on others.

Every organisation has established norms of behaviour. There is always a reason for such norms, even if the reason has long ago become irrelevant, and even if the reason is patently absurd. The pressures on individuals to conform to standards of corporate behaviour, rather than hold true to their own beliefs are overwhelming: rare is the individual who does not bend.

In a building society, a branch manager was demoted by being transferred to a smaller branch. He had consistently failed to meet his sales 'targets'. He continued to fail at the new branch. It was only when the recession resulted in spiralling bad debt and house repossessions that management discovered that he had the best record in the society for quality of lending and customer retention.

The greatest barriers to Total Quality are to be found in a company's mechanisms for motivation and reward. This seldom has anything much to do with pay. For most people, the influence of management's expectations is infinitely more powerful than what the customer expects. The requirement is to align management's objectives with meeting the needs of customers.

Total Quality means continuous improvement of every aspect of an organisation's operations at the fastest pace that the people in it can sustain. It includes every activity, every decision, every element of behaviour by every employee. This brings to quality a very human dimension, and presents severe challenges to our traditional thinking on management.

Organisations are full of dedicated people – people who, in their spare time, run scout troops, do voluntary work, are champion gardeners, and so forth. They are full of dedication and motivation, except when they are at work. The challenge is to harness that latent dedication, involvement and excitement in working hours as well as in leisure time.

It is easy to blame management, trapped in a way of managing that can be traced back to the early days of the industrial revolution. Much of our management thinking has been based on the influence of Frederick Winslow Taylor, an American born in 1856. Taylor is best known for his work in Bethlehem Steel where, by organising workers' efforts, he was able to more than double their efficiency. He was the first productivity expert.

But Taylor's approach had a darker side. In his book, *Industrial Utopia*, he uses phrases such as:

'Under our system a worker is told just what to do and how he is to do it. Any improvement he makes upon the orders given to him is fatal to his success.'

> 'Hardly a competent workman can be found who does not devote a considerable amount of time studying just how slowly he can work and still convince his employer that he is going at a good pace'.

Echoes of Taylor still permeate Western management thinking. Taylor did not expect workers to think – he saw that as the duty of management alone. In his world, workers supplied only their labour, and were considered expendable – a resource no different from machines. It is hardly surprising that workers responded to management indifference by creating trade unions. Thus were the conventional roles for managers and workers cast.

Taylor's productivity revolution dehumanised labour. Total Quality rehumanises. It encourages people to think, to develop to their full potential and to maximise the contribution they can make to the organisation.

To illustrate the potential, contrast the participation achieved by many Japanese manufacturing companies where it is common for averages of between 100 and 600 ideas for change to be generated each year by each employee, 95 per cent of which are implemented! This is the single greatest advantage that the Japanese have over us. They have found a way of managing that liberates the full potential of their people.

The common sense principles

To many, a first reading of the basic principles of Total Quality comes across as plain common sense. The perception is accurate. The point is that these things simply don't happen in most companies. They are:

- prevention not correction;
- continuous improvement;
- process management;
- constancy of purpose;
- leadership by example;
- involvement of everyone;
- right first time, every time;
- quality is not a cost;
- customer focus.

Prevention not correction

It is self-evident that if we prevent failure, we eliminate the cost of correcting it. Sometimes the cost of correction can be so high that it literally threatens the business.

A software company discovered that more than 80 per cent of its development resources were devoted to fixing bugs in its products installed on customer sites. They calculated that the cost of fixing errors in a software product in the field was 2,000 times the cost of correcting them before the product was released. They were forced to freeze product development and spend 8 months retesting existing products before reinstalling them free of charge at all customer sites. The company then re-engineered the whole development process to design quality into their products in the first place.

Managers are often respected for their ability to 'fight fires'. The problem is that fire fighting is a random technique. Sometimes, by pure luck, the root cause of the problem is addressed and a genuine improvement is made. But all too often, the use of gut feel and emotion leads to treatment of the symptoms, not the disease. As a result, symptoms reappear – often different ones, and usually more painful than the last.

The matrix in Figure 1 illustrates that in any process of change, true improvement only occurs when two conditions are met:

Figure 1 *Achieving true improvement*

	Change was a bad idea	Change was a good idea
Change was poorly planned or executed	**Inefficient waste**	**Missed opportunity**
Change was well planned and executed	**Efficient waste**	**True improvement**

- when the change is a good idea – that is, when the root cause of a problem is being addressed by the best solution;
- when that change is well planned and executed.

In our experience, the most common flaw is failure to identify the root cause of the problem. This is almost invariably because the cause is elsewhere in the organisation, beyond the immediate authority of those who suffer its effects. A customer accounts department that must raise a credit note is seldom responsible for the problem that triggered the need to give money back to the customer in the first place.

Continuous improvement

'If it ain't broke, don't fix it' precludes the possibility of improvement. Continuous improvement means that everyone has an attitude of never being satisfied that something is being done well enough. That something could be tangible, such as a product or an aspect of service, or it could be less tangible, such as improving teamwork, working to break down interfunctional barriers or the coaching of people to improve their capability.

In companies where real advances in Total Quality have been achieved this attitude has become a healthy *obsession*.

Process management

Organisations are vertical structures, but processes operate horizontally. Central to this principle is the notion that every activity is part of a cross-functional process. Everyone is at one time or another both a supplier of a service and a customer. Some suppliers and customers are external to the company, but many are internal. Business processes bind activities together in chains of internal supplier/customer relationships.

To maximise the efficiency and effectiveness of the overall process, managers have to learn to work cross-functionally to improve processes. After many years of working in functional gold fish bowls, such changes do not come easily.

Constancy of purpose

The commitment to quality must begin with top management, and then be transmitted throughout the organisation. Quality is not optional. Everybody must have a common view of the company's goals, and of how they are to be achieved.

This means communication. There is however a fundamental difference between communication and merely disseminating information. It is not enough for management to release memoranda, newsletters and videos stating the company's commitment to Total Quality and customer care.

> *An insurance company established an internal communication unit whose remit was to maintain a thorough process of staff communications in support of a Total Quality initiative. The company published its mission statement and objectives, policy documents, a monthly newspaper, regular newsletters for every major quality improvement project, videos on controversial topics and frequent briefing notes from the board. When they subsequently surveyed staff on the effectiveness of company communications, they were appalled to find that they perceived communication to be worse than before. Staff saw it all as concentrated propaganda: they were being shouted at, not communicated with.*

Communication is a two-way process that involves listening. Otherwise, it is mere exhortation. More importantly, it must be face-to-face. Even effective personal communication will be undermined if management behaviour then contradicts the message. Removing fear involves building trust.

Leadership by example

Defining Total Quality as a system of behaviour implies that there must be a set of norms for behaviour that everybody can follow. In any organisation, those at the top are role models for everyone else.

Leadership and good behaviour don't necessarily go together. Hitler, Mussolini, Stalin and Saddam Hussein – to take a few well-known recent examples – can all be described as strong leaders, and it is easy to identify autocratic and dictatorial leaders of companies. Autocracy is an easy way to fill a leadership vacuum, and in the short term, dictators can get things done: Mussolini is said to have got the trains to run on time, although this is probably apocryphal. It is much more likely that people *told* him they were running on time, and even more likely that *he* told *them* they were running on time.

Autocracy may breed 'strong' leaders. But it also breeds something else: fear. Fear takes many forms, and in working life it extends from fear of losing one's job, through fear of personal failure to fear of blame or criticism.

Many companies have a 'fear culture'. It does not depend on aggression or rudeness, but it exists wherever there is lack of trust. Many senior managers are horrified to discover that their subordinates fear them, because as individuals they do not intend it or actively encourage it.

> *The managing director of a bank accepted the existence of a fear culture when it was pointed out to him that in a meeting with a group of junior staff, everybody developed a liking for black coffee with no sugar: he was seated between all of them and the milk and sugar.*

Fear should never be confused with respect, and deference is a dangerous sign. The newly appointed chief executive of a financial services company described the culture he found as 'long on deference and short on respect'.

Few people are 'natural leaders'. Natural leaders have vision, commitment, drive and charisma, and they are few and far between. But leadership can be learnt and others can lead effectively by concentrating on behaviour that generates trust and encourages teamwork.

It is demonstrably possible to develop a climate of leadership, by removing the barriers to cooperation and trust, and by encouraging and rewarding teamwork. The key capability of a manager should be his or her ability to foster teamwork.

Involvement of everyone

Piecemeal attempts to improve quality seldom succeed, for two important reasons. Business processes cross all functions, and involve people at all levels in the organisation: a business process is only as effective as its weakest link. Perhaps more importantly, as a system of behaviour Total Quality represents a permanent change in the culture of the whole organisation.

> *A clearing bank invested heavily in a customer care programme and information technology for its front office staff. It neglected the back office where most of the routine processing was done. The result was that some of the hard-earned improvements in customer perceptions were dissipated by errors in the back office caused by poorly trained and motivated staff, and inadequate systems. More significantly, the customer care programme itself fell into disrepute.*

Right first time, every time

It is an obvious truth that nobody goes to work deliberately to make mistakes. Yet in every business, hundreds or even thousands of errors are made every day. Studies consistently show that 20 to 40 per cent of all activity in an organisation is wasted: fire fighting, resolving queries, redoing work only because a task was not done right the first time.

People do, however, make mistakes. There are six reasons why mistakes happen:

1 too little *time* to do the job properly;
2 inadequate *training*;
3 inappropriate or inadequate *tools*;
4 incomplete, missing or inaccurate *information*;
5 faulty *material* to work on;
6 human error.

All but the last are the responsibility of management, and therefore outside the control of employees working within a process.

We have omitted two other factors that are commonly seen as the reason for mistakes and failure: incompetence and poor motivation. Incompetence implies innate inability to do a particular task. Such an individual should not be recruited to that task, or should be removed from it when his or her incompetence becomes known. These are also management responsibilities, and not a matter for personal blame on the individual – who may have other talents.

Poor motivation can be personal – related to an individual's domestic circumstances or, rarely, to his or her personality. We discuss the subject of motivation in Chapter 6. It is enough here to say that in any organisation, staff motivation is predominantly the consequence of the organisation's culture and mechanisms of incentive and reward, and these remain the responsibility of management.

So in almost all cases, the cause of mistakes in an organisation can be traced back to managers, not to those whom they manage. Telling people to do their job right first time without providing them with the necessary support is merely exhortation. All exhortation ever achieves is to create a climate of fear and mistrust of management.

A manufacturing company acquired the assets and property of a failed competitor. Its managers found a number of quality posters which they put up in their own factory. The workers' initial reaction was derision, followed by contempt. They had to work with antiquated, poorly-maintained equipment. They were not deliberately producing poor quality. Management were responsible for that.

11

Posters have a place, but only when management has invested in resources that allow people to do a quality job and take pride in their work. This is a right that management owes to every employee.

Quality is not a cost

The simplest but most misunderstood quality principle is that enhancing quality is not a cost. In many companies, the costs of poor quality (checking, correcting and reworking other peoples' work, scrap, and so forth) amount to between 20 and 40 per cent of sales. Doing it right first time, thereby eliminating this waste, is *always* a lesser cost. This is what Crosby[3] means when he states that 'quality is free'. Furthermore, organisations not only save the cost of putting right what should have been done right first time, the time saved reduces cycle and response times, and frees resources to add value.

> *Mercedes Benz employed a group of craftsmen whose task it was to check every vehicle coming off the production line, and to put right any faults they found. The company discovered that it expended more labour hours per vehicle on this rectification activity than Toyota needed to build a Lexus right first time.*

Quality should not be confused with a high *specification*; nor does it mean producing what the customer is unwilling to pay for. Even delighted customers are cost conscious.

Understanding the relationship between cost and quality is critically important. Conventional approaches to cost management tend to focus on the cost of a resource, not on the activities carried out by that resource. In Chapter 7 we discuss in more detail three types of activity – core, support and diversionary. Core activity adds value; support activity (such as filing or travel) does not itself add value, but is needed to enable core activity to take place; diversionary activity is the consequence of process failure. Effective cost management involves understanding where diversionary activities are taking place, tracking back to their root causes, and preventing recurrence.

Customer focus

Constancy of purpose and process management are meaningless without a focus on the customers' requirements. Processes have no meaning without customers. Therefore process improvement must be guided by a clear understanding of customer requirements and perceptions. We discuss this subject in detail in Chapter 4.

The responsibility for customer focus starts with top management emphasis on the organisation's external customer: ensuring that both requirements and perceptions are understood product group by product group, market segment by market segment; and that gaps and deficiencies are identified, resources made available and directed, and priorities set.

The next level of emphasis is on the needs of internal customers – establishing requirements, measuring performance, identifying areas for improvement.

Customers' requirements are dynamic. Failing to understand how requirements are changing causes improvement efforts to be misdirected, and less important aspects of customer requirements to be emphasised at the expense of customers' most important needs.

Kaizen – The key to Japan's success

Thousands of Western managers have visited Japan to understand the secret of its success. There is, however, no secret to find. The Japanese are disarmingly open about their management practices, which are simple to understand but radically different from traditional Western management practice.

One of the myths about Japan is that everything is run super-efficiently. One trip to the Narita airport outside Tokyo is enough to disabuse anyone of that notion. Poorly designed, with long queues and a high level of bureaucracy, it compares very unfavourably with many US and European airports. But just outside the airport, the best of Japan can be seen.

> *A traveller to Japan arrived via several other countries, having collected a variety of foreign bank notes that he wanted to exchange for Yen. The bureau de change insisted on a separate form for each currency. Each form required identical information: name, address, passport number and so forth – tiresome and unnecessary bureaucracy after a long flight. A few days later, he wanted to travel by train to a Tokyo suburb: he asked his hosts how to read the name of the station so he knew when to get off. He was told not to worry, simply to get off the train when his watch told him the time was 12:28. British Rail please copy.*

Such contrasts are visible throughout Japan. There are some ferociously efficient and competitive companies. There are others that are just as poorly managed as any in the West. The point of this is not that there is something

13

fundamentally Japanese about quality, but that there are good and bad approaches to management.

The best of Japan's management practice is embodied in the approach called *Kaizen* (Ky'zen). The word is derived from two other words. 'Kai' which means 'change', and 'Zen' which means 'good' (for the better). Hence 'Kaizen' translates eventually to continuous improvement. Kaizen is one of the most commonly used words in Japan. News broadcasts speak of the Kaizen of Japan's trade balance. The word is firmly embedded in the Japanese working culture.

Kaizen is not a single approach. Rather, it is an umbrella for a larger number of techniques which include for example:

- quality circles;
- suggestion schemes;
- robotics;
- automation;
- just-in-time;
- total preventive maintenance;
- Kanban;
- zero defects;
- industrial relations;
- productivity improvements;
- statistics;
- graphs.

Kaizen and management

Kaizen identifies two aspects of management: *improvement* and *maintenance*. The Japanese expect Kaizen to represent an average of 50 per cent of management time, with differing emphasis on either improvement or maintenance at different levels in the hierarchy.

Maintenance means activities directed at sustaining current levels of performance, for example through training. Improvement is directed at improving levels of performance. The Japanese perception of management simply boils down to a single concept: a continuous cycle of maintaining and improving standards.

Within *maintenance*, management's role is to establish what procedures are to be followed to ensure that everyone is capable – that is, trained to follow the procedure. The standard is maintained by rigorous training, particularly on the job; and by discipline.

Table 1

Western emphasis	Kaizen emphasis
Innovation.	Innovation balanced with incremental improvement.
Big steps.	Small steps in large numbers.
Invest to improve.	Best efforts to improve existing technology.
Technology.	Conventional knowledge.
Results-oriented.	Process-oriented.

Lasting improvement is only acheived when people work to ever higher standards. *Improvement* means improving the standard. Once that has been done, management's task is to maintain the improved standard, and so the cycle of ever-improving standards is maintained.

Improvement can be divided into innovation and incremental improvement. In the West, we have become obsessed with innovation – the big breakthrough, the latest investment in technology, the next new product.

Kaizen has a different emphasis. Innovation is carefully balanced by incremental improvement – small steps using people's knowledge and conventional know-how.

Process orientation compared with results orientation

In Kaizen, the process (action plan) is considered as important as the intended result. By contrast, Western companies traditionally focus strongly on the end result, while the process by which the result is to be achieved often receives little attention.

Sumo wrestling illustrates result and process thinking. In a tournament, there are three prizes in addition to the tournament prize: an outstanding performance award, a skill award and a fighting spirit award. These awards may be won even if the wrestler has lost every bout.

Process orientation has a strong emphasis on people. A Kaizen manager will be keenly interested in discipline, morale, communication, and the attitude, participation and involvement of all his people. A results-oriented manager controls his people by reward and penalty, with emphasis on individual performance.

15

Use of data

Kaizen places great emphasis on problem-solving techniques and statistical tools, the vast majority of which are extremely simple. A visitor to almost any Japanese factory would see these tools in routine use by any employee, either individually or in small group activities. Graphic displays of problems, trends and cause and effect relationships would be everywhere.

Japanese executives apply a technique refined by Deming known as PDCA (Plan, Do, Check, Act) in any situation. The cycle begins with an understanding of the current situation in which data is collected as a basis for formulating a plan of action. Once implemented, the effects of the plan are verified to ensure that the desired outcome has been achieved. As a final stage, the new method is standardised to hold the gain.

By following the PDCA cycle routinely, managers make decisions based on fact, not intuition. PDCA is not so much a technique but a basic behaviour to be used in any decision-making or important situation.

Kaizen hierarchy

Kaizen describes clear roles for all levels of management and staff in an organisation.

For top management, Kaizen means providing resources and direction, as well as defining the Kaizen strategy. Middle managers' job is to deploy that strategy, to use improvement tools and techniques to implement the strategy, and to establish and maintain standards. Supervisors' main role is to participate in and encourage small group activities – to lead them in doing the work.

Kaizen is highly people-oriented. It is based on the conviction that everyone can contribute significantly to improving his or her own workplace, given the right encouragement, support and training. It presupposes that most people want to take pride in their work and want to improve both the quality of their work and their personal capability. This desire is not unique to Japan, and therefore the Kaizen concept is as valid in other countries as it is there. Concepts such as focus on the customer, cross-functional management, PDCA, policy deployment and problem-solving are all part of Kaizen and relevant to any enterprise, anywhere.

Table 2 *The Kaizen hierarchy*[A]

Top management	Middle management	Supervisors	People
Be determined to introduce Kaizen as a corporate strategy	Deploy and implement Kaizen goals as directed through policy deployment and cross-functional management	Use Kaizen in daily work	Engage in Kaizen
Provide support and direction by allocating resources	Use Kaizen in functional capabilities	Formulate plans for Kaizen and provide guidance to workers	Practice discipline
Establish policy for Kaizen and cross-functional goals	Establish, maintain, improve standards	Improve communications with workers and sustain morale	Engage in continuous self-improvement
Realise goals through policy deployment	Make people Kaizen-conscious	Support small-group activities and suggestions scheme	Enhance skills and job performance
Build systems, processes conducive to Kaizen	Support people in developing skills and tools	Maintain discipline	Generate Kaizen suggestions
		Generate Kaizen suggestions	

The success of Kaizen cannot be disputed. The challenge to Western management is clear. We must throw away much of what we have learned about management whether from business school or practical experience. The greatest barrier to continuous improvement is not people. It is management practice.

CHAPTER 2

The structure and foundations of Total Quality

'Change is difficult: those who stand to lose will resist it, while those who stand to gain don't know it yet.'

Machiavelli

In Chapter 1 we described what is meant by Total Quality, and contrasted the best of Japanese management practice with the conventional approach to management in the West. We also stressed that there is nothing uniquely Japanese about Total Quality, and there is much in the best of Western management practice that provides the opportunity to learn.

Perhaps the most repeated advice about Total Quality is that it is not a project – it is a journey without end. Wouldn't it be nice to arrive, and put your feet up? People – especially results-oriented managers – like projects: they have an end, a result. There is something rather daunting about change that goes on forever.

It is not that people are resistant to change *per se*. We are all resistant to change imposed by others, particularly when experience tells us that it is likely to be in their interest, not in ours. Total Quality implies that everyone in the organisation is involved in a process of continuous change – voluntarily, because they see it to be in their own interest.

The structure of Total Quality

Total Quality has a coherent structure, with three main components – behavioural, management and technical.

The *behavioural component* is concerned with building an environment in which people can realise their full potential through mutual trust, respect and

Figure 2 The structure of Total Quality

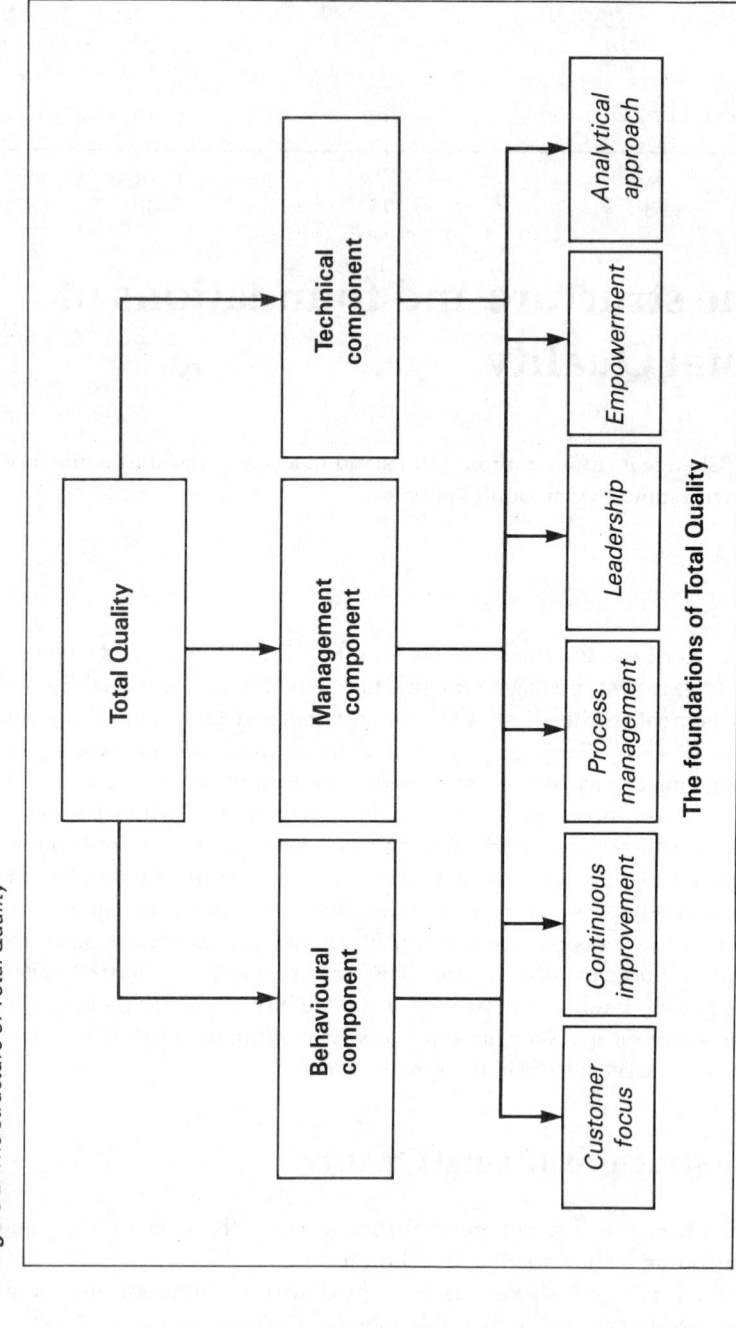

support between management and staff. Top managers must take the lead by demonstrating their personal commitment to continuous improvement. This can be done by effective communication based on listening, and, crucially, through their personal behaviour. When management behaves in a manner consistent with the values and beliefs implicit in Total Quality, then and only then can they expect their people to change their behaviour.

The *management component* is the infrastructure of Total Quality. It includes top management's vision for the organisation and the role Total Quality is to play. It also includes the establishment of agreed goals and measures at every level of the organisation and the consistency of functional and individual goals with the overall goals of the organisation.

The *technical component* is a structured approach to problem-solving based on data collection, a disciplined approach to problem prevention, and the use of generally simple statistical and graphical tools. It also includes tools to assist in identifying the voice of the customer, design of experiments, reducing cycle times, and the conduct of meetings.

Many companies make the mistake of over-emphasising the technical component. The key is behavioural change. Even in the management and technical components, behaviour is critical. The rigorous deployment of goals and measures of performance for all levels of an organisation is primarily behavioural, as is the personal discipline required to make routine use of analytical tools and techniques.

Table 3

Behavioural component	Management component	Technical component
Is our behaviour – both individual and group – well-adapted to the new way of working and thinking?	Is the improvement process well-directed by leaders? Are systems and structures well-adapted for reinforcing Total Quality?	Are we applying the right tools and techniques in the improvement process?

Underpinning this structure are the six foundations of Total Quality:

1 customer focus;
2 continuous improvement;
3 process management;
4 leadership;
5 empowerment;
6 analytical approach.

Foundation one: customer focus

The purpose of any organisation and the focus of everyone's efforts should be to serve the needs of its customers. This means that the organisation must monitor how its external customer requirements may be changing, and how customers perceive the quality of its products and services in relation to those of its competitors.

It is of course essential, but seldom enough, for a product to be fit for its declared purpose.

> *On a drizzly day in Oxford Street a street trader was selling umbrellas at a price that was, as he put it, a very pleasant surprise. Business was brisk until a passer-by stopped to announce that he had bought one of the umbrellas the day before. He was, he said, delighted with both the price and the way it went up at the push of a button. His only complaint was that, once up, the rain came straight through it.*

A product should also have performance characteristics: the more these are present, the greater the customer satisfaction. The competitive advantage that they offer tends to be temporary, until the competition can emulate them. A good example is increasing fuel economy and performance in motor cars.

There are also characteristics of products and services that are *distinctive*. Such characteristics provide something the customer did not expect, but nonetheless appreciates. Distinctive characteristics can be very easy to find.

> *A British traveller arrived at a hotel in the US, and tried to buy a British newspaper in its shop. The assistant apologised that she had sold the last copy. Twenty minutes later, The Times was delivered to his room: she had asked the bell captain to send someone to the next hotel to buy one for him.*

A delighted customer. In Chapter 4 we discuss delighting customers further.

Foundation two: continuous improvement

Total Quality depends on continuous, incremental change and innovation initiated at all levels in the organisation – not on periodic radical change initiated from above.

This is well illustrated by the subtle but critically important difference between 'cost cutting' and 'cost reduction'. 'Cost cutting' refers to any management practice aimed at removing costs rapidly, which usually involves people losing their jobs. By contrast, 'cost reduction' describes a *continuous* process of cost elimination. By improving profitability, cost reduction is a means of *creating* jobs. The logic is straightforward: unless a company continually reduces the cost of developing, producing and delivering products and services to meet the changing needs of its customers, it will become uncompetitive. Furthermore, cost reduction should not be seen as a 'management' practice, but one that all staff are engaged in.

> *In a presentation to a group of visitors from the UK, a Japanese brewery showed a chart of the number of its employees, which had fallen by two-thirds over a period of 10 years. The visitors asked how this was compatible with their policy of lifetime employment. Their hosts did not at first understand the question. When they did, they explained that during the same period, the company had opened six other breweries in Japan and that total company employment had doubled.*

In Chapter 6 we examine the nature of change, and discuss some of the main barriers to incremental change.

Foundation three: process management

Activities in an organisation are not undertaken in isolation; something, such as a request for information or the receipt of a sales order, triggers them. The activity generates an output which in turn prompts others to begin different activities.

Collectively, events which are linked together in this way form a business process. Business processes are the life-blood of any organisation: their summation defines its operations.

A key feature of business processes is that they invariably travel *across* the organisation, involving people from many different departments.

For the company to work cohesively and efficiently, it is necessary that these business processes operate smoothly. But this requires close coordination of the departments through which the processes run. In all but the smallest companies, management parochialism prevents this happening as walls are erected between different parts of the organisation.

It has been estimated that 90 per cent of all process problems have their root causes at the barriers between departments.

Figure 3 *Business processes*

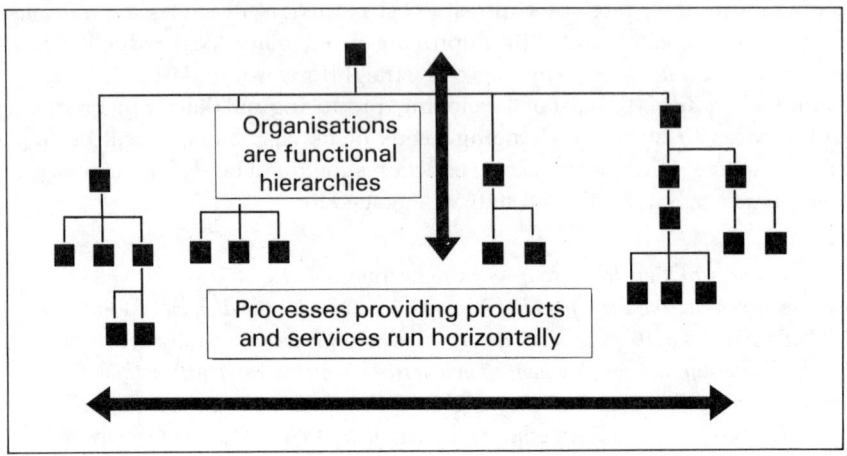

Staff see only the part of the process that passes through their area of control. Blind to the perspective of the overall process, they have neither the knowledge nor the authority to improve it. Moreover, the process is not coordinated from one end to the other, and there is little understanding of the link between poor performance of the process and the effect this has on the level of service it provides to its customer – frequently an external customer.

In Chapters 5 and 6 we discuss the barriers to cross-functional cooperation; and Chapter 7 includes practical ways of implementing process management.

Foundation four: leadership

Total Quality starts at the executive level and cascades down through the whole organisation. It is a strategic rather than an operational commitment made by top management that they be the driving force behind the transformation of their business through Total Quality. When management make that commitment they commit themselves to practice what they preach.

To start with, top management must be committed to a positive answer to the following questions:

- Are you willing to undertake a process of learning that will challenge many of your preconceived notions of good management practice?
- Are you willing to change your personal behaviour?
- Are you willing to support and coach your people through a similar journey of self-discovery?

- Will you demonstrate your commitment by your actions?
- Are you willing to be patient?

It is possible to feel slightly sorry for top managers: people are always telling them that this or that initiative 'requires their total commitment'. What is it that they are actually expected to *do?*

The first step is intensive education and learning, a large part of which is 'unlearning'. It is impossible to be committed without knowledge and understanding of what Total Quality is, and what the implications are for the organisation. This also needs to be inspirational – commitment is emotive, and a little passion is not misplaced. It is no coincidence that those who have made progress with quality stand in what Sir Ralph Richardson once described as a 'little puddle of pride' when they describe to others what their businesses have been able to achieve.

In this book we focus a great deal on the role of management (Chapter 5), and on the barriers to developing a Total Quality culture (Chapter 6). It is an organisation's leadership that determines the role of management, and has the authority to break down the barriers. It is also top management's responsibility to set Total Quality within the necessary strategic perspective, and we discuss this further in the next chapter.

Foundation five: empowerment

Like 'leadership', 'empowerment' is a much misunderstood word. It is not the same as delegation.

> *The managing director of a leading electronics company issued a memo that described his personal commitment to empowerment, and formally delegated authority for different types of decision down the management hierarchy. Nothing happened. People continued to refer decisions upwards, in contravention of his instructions. Managers in the hierarchy saw the change as a threat to their authority, and refused to trust subordinates with decisions they had previously regarded as their own. Staff lacked the confidence to take decisions for fear of blame or contradiction by their managers.*

Telling people they are empowered changes nothing. Empowerment is an inner feeling. People feel empowered when they believe they are valued by the organisation, and when there is no threat of penalty or blame for a wrong decision.

Empowerment cannot exist unless managers see their role as one of *supporting* their staff, not *controlling* them. We discuss empowerment in greater detail in Chapter 5.

Foundation six: analytical approach

Most managers spend their time dealing with the past – firefighting, crisis management and so forth. This is little more than patchwork management. We should really be spending our time looking forward, managing the future.

> *Recently, a large American automotive company carried out an analysis to compare the amount of time its managers spent managing problems generated in the past with time spent on the challenges of the future. They found that the past occupied 80 per cent of their time. A similar benchmark was carried out in cooperation with a Japanese competitor. The results were almost exactly transposed.*

How much more efficient and competitive could businesses be if management's efforts were directed at tackling the competition rather than sorting out historical problems?

If you ask a manager how to improve quality, he is likely to mention:

- computers;
- automation;
- investment in new technology;
- work measurement;
- benchmarking;
- performance-related pay and incentives;
- profit-sharing;
- business process re-engineering;
- performance appraisal.

Ask what his experience of these things has been in the past, and the answer is almost invariably disappointment (and it was always someone else's fault). Why is this the case? A key reason is that managers make decisions without sufficient *knowledge*. Lacking it, they are unable to predict an outcome. Without prediction, we increase the possibility of making the wrong decisions; or we make the right decisions without fully understanding the implications, and fail to obtain the full benefits; or we maintain an imperfect status quo by lacking the confidence to make a decision at all.

Faced with a board submission for capital expenditure on new CNC machine tools, the chief executive of a manufacturing company initiated a review of all capital expenditure made by production engineering. The review showed that if the total of all cost savings projected as a result of capital expenditure over the previous five years had been delivered, the company would have achieved a negative manufacturing cost.

Three aspects of knowledge are significant: variation, interdependencies and prediction.

Knowledge of variation

All business processes contain variation. Some is natural variation which occurs in even the most robustly designed process: this is described as variation due to *common causes*, and is statistically predictable. Other variation has *special causes*, so named because they are not present all the time. Special causes tend to have significant effects. For example, a new employee will, through lack of knowledge or training, be a special cause of variation in a process, with the result that quality of output and efficiency are likely to suffer until he or she is fully experienced.

Managers need knowledge of variation in order to distinguish between common and special causes. A process in which all variation is due to common causes is said to be 'in statistical control' – that is, predictable and consistent in the quality it produces.

Continuous improvement can be thought of as a never-ending battle against variation – a process of identifying the root causes of variation, preventing recurrence and thereby gradually improving the robustness of the whole process.

The whole subject of variation is outside the scope of this book, and is well worth special study. Appendix D contains suggested further reading. In particular, Deming[5] provides much useful insight into variation and the theory of knowledge. Mal Owen's book, *SPC and Continuous Improvement*[6], is a thorough practical guide on the subject.

Knowledge of interdependencies

Our organisations have become increasingly complex. Lack of robustness in a process can be caused by many elements: people, systems, procedures, organisation, or a combination of any or all of these. As organisations grow, the number of people and departments increases, multiplying the number of interactions and interdependencies. Managers need knowledge of these interdependencies to track back to the root causes of process failures and to increase overall effectiveness.

Prediction

Every management decision involves prediction. Therefore any decision made without the best knowledge available is based on inadequate prediction, and the decision itself becomes less likely to be the right one. This is not to devalue judgement and flair, and decisions made with the best of knowledge can be wrong. Nevertheless, whatever can be done to improve the probability of good decisions provides the opportunity for competitive advantage.

The 'tools and techniques' of Total Quality are aimed at supporting an analytical approach to problem-solving and process improvement. They are outlined in Appendix A. Their use should become routine, and a matter of thorough training for everyone in the organisation.

CHAPTER 3

Positioning and capability

'Two explorers were trudging across the icy wastes. Suddenly a polar bear reared up from behind a glacier.

"What do we do now?" asked one of the men.

The other man knelt down, removed his snow shoes and took a pair of trainers out of his knapsack.

"It's pointless putting those on," said the first man, "those bears can outrun any man."

"I know," said the other, "but I only have to run faster than you."'

Old joke

Positioning and capability are twinned concepts that are remarkably powerful in helping organisations to set Total Quality within the appropriate strategic context. In particular they are concepts that help grapple with the problems of how best to direct resources. In this chapter we describe what is meant by positioning and capability, discuss the principles and issues underpinning them and give some examples of the use to which they should be put.

Positioning is to do with external factors: which products and services are we selling to whom; what are our customers' needs; who are our competitors and how do we compare with them; what is the legislative framework; what do our shareholders expect?

Capability covers internal factors: do we have the necessary technology and skills; do we have the *right* competence; are our business processes capable of consistently meeting customers' expectations for quality products and services, or do they permit failures to occur; is our organisation responsive; how well do we innovate; does our culture help us or hinder us?

Some companies focus inwards, developing their capability without understanding what their customers need or what their competitors are doing. Others focus outwards, positioning themselves in order to set objectives their business processes are incapable of meeting and creating customer expectations they cannot satisfy.

Positioning and capability are inextricably linked; organisations must work on both at the same time.

The journey

In setting out to create a company's own future, many factors will influence the direction, the route and the means of getting there. Moreover, the journey (Figure 4) is iterative, with continuous checks and modifications on the way. This means building into the company's information and accounting systems the feedback that management need to manage the process of change. Management information must therefore include *prediction* that describes both the future positioning the company wants to achieve, and the capability needed to deliver it. Such prediction must not be limited to the financial consequences, but must focus on the factors that generate them.

Customers have differing needs: can the company identify the specific and different internal capabilities that will meet those needs? Does the company have a clear plan for its own actions in relation to the competition, for every type of product, for every type of customer? Does the company have an organisation that can respond to the plan, or is the organisation itself a barrier to changing positioning and enhancing capability? Does the company know where it is on the journey, and what to do next?

Answering these questions requires a clear understanding of three elements within the strategy:

1 product/customer segmentation by *common capability*;
2 competitive stance;
3 organisational classification.

Figure 4 *The journey*

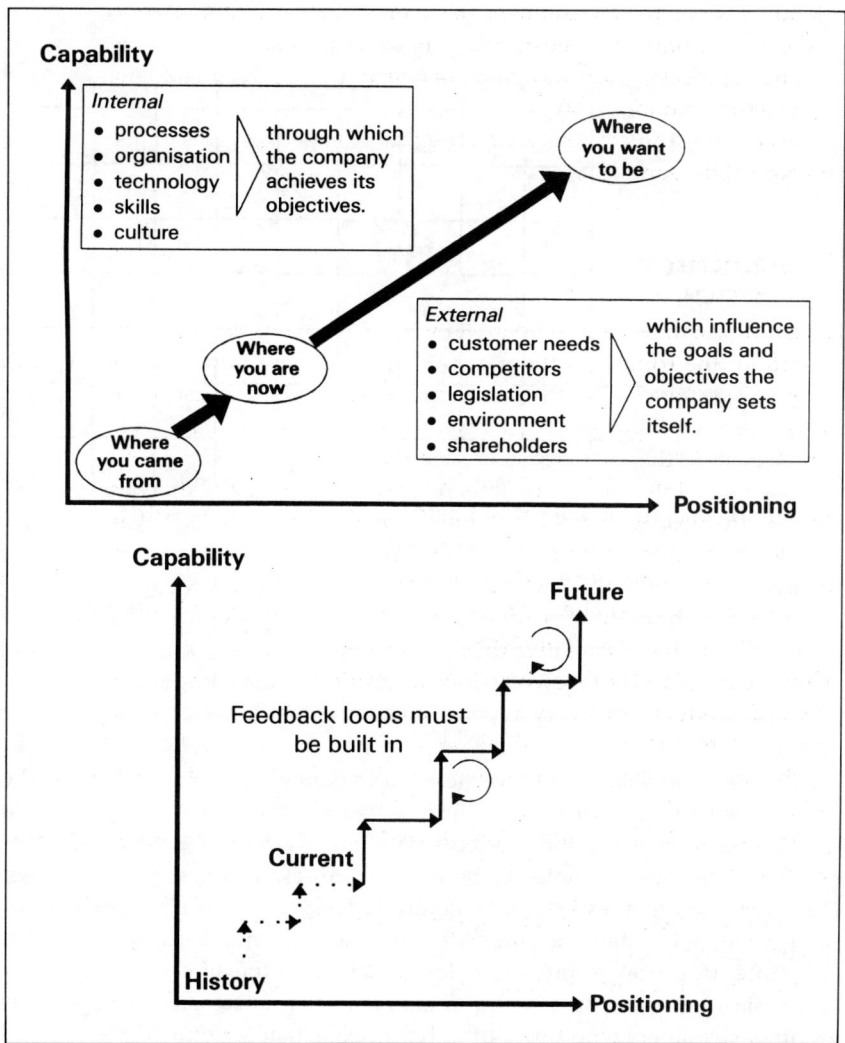

Product/customer segmentation by common capability

Figure 5 illustrates a product/customer segmentation based on common capability. The shaded area links all the products and customer groups that have *common processes from the sales channel through to customer after-care*.

Figure 5 *Product/customer segmentation*

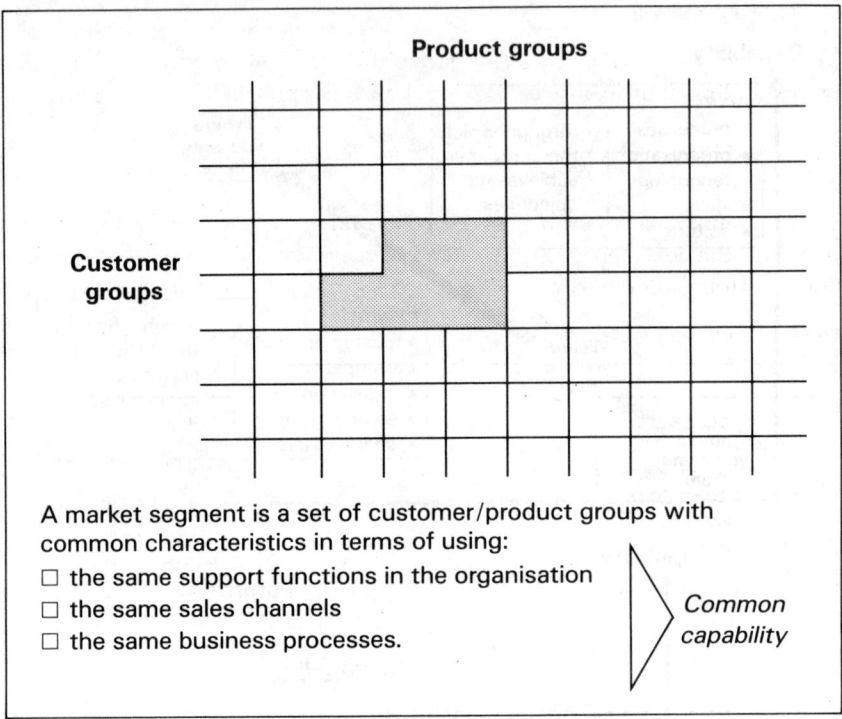

Product groups

Customer groups

A market segment is a set of customer/product groups with common characteristics in terms of using:
- ☐ the same support functions in the organisation
- ☐ the same sales channels
- ☐ the same business processes.

Common capability

Extending the shaded area vertically brings new customer groups to the process; extending it horizontally introduces new products or new services to the process. Increasing the shaded area is an advantage because it enables existing skills and resources to be applied to new business opportunities. However, careful investigation is required to ensure that the new product or service does not contaminate the service to customers on existing products. If it does, internal processes must be redesigned to meet the different needs.

A typical trap companies fall into is to market existing products to a new group of customers who turn out to have needs that are quite different, and beyond the capability of the existing process.

> *When a bank introduced a TESSA it offered a telephone enquiry service on the same charge-free telephone number that it used for other products. Although the operators were given the necessary technical training to answer questions from potential customers, the switchboard capacity was inadequate; by*

overstretching its capability, potential customers of all products, not just the TESSA, suffered.

Completing the matrix is seldom straightforward. It requires a thorough understanding of the company's internal business processes.

Competitive stance

Having defined the company's current and potential product/customer segments, the next step is to understand its *competitive stance* on each. Figure 6 illustrates four different competitive stances – *new, nurture, defend,* and *steal*.

Figure 6 Competitive stance

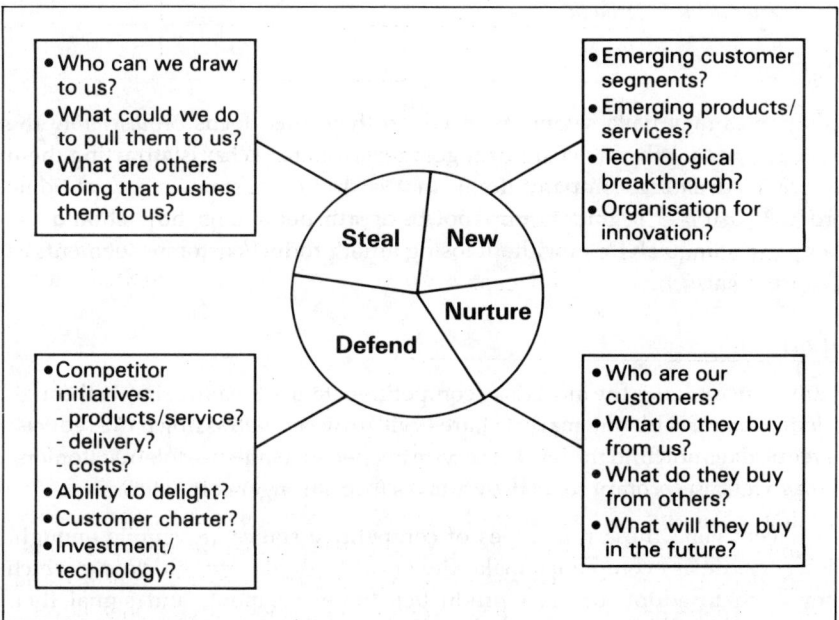

New

A segment may be *new*, created by marketing existing products to a new customer group, or, conversely, by marketing new products to an existing group. The new segment may be based on a technological breakthrough, which delivers lower unit cost or an improved product/service specification, or on the emergence of a new potential market such as Eastern Europe.

Nurture

The competitive stance may be to cross-sell current or new products to existing customers – 'nurturing' the existing customer base. This is not cynical exploitation: it means customers buying more from a company because of its record of product and service quality. In order to be able to nurture its existing customer base, a company must know who its customers are and what they buy from it and from its competitors. It must develop an assessment of what they are likely to buy in the future.

> A senior executive of British Telecom is reported to have observed that, at the time of privatisation, the only thing that BT knew about its customers was their telephone number, a lack of knowledge that presented a significant barrier to future growth.

Defend

Companies may have segments in which they must focus on *defending* the customer base. Why are customers going elsewhere? What is attracting them away? What is the company doing that is driving customers away? Some product/customer segments may not be worth defending: how should the company relinquish them without losing other product/customer segments as a consequence?

Steal

Stealing customers is the most risky competitive stance. Stealing simply through price reduction – buying market share – will prove embarrassing if the reduced revenue does not fund the level of service needed to retain the stolen customers. It may well also prompt retaliatory attacks from stronger competitors.

Conceptually, these four types of competitive stance are simple enough. However, unless companies make the effort to think through clearly which they wish to adopt for each product/customer segment, and signal their intentions throughout the organisation, there will be endless confusion and wasted effort.

Organisational classification

Having positioned the company by defining its customer/product segments, and having decided which competitive stance is needed, the next step is to examine how the organisation itself can deliver the necessary capability.

Delivering capability is not the simple mechanistic task that some managers believe. Norms of organisational behaviour become deep-seated and extraordinarily powerful. If altering capability demands a change in these norms, it will be a major task. If the organisation fails to recognise the type of barriers it faces, its attempts to change will founder.

In order to recognise these barriers, it is useful to think of four major types of organisation:

- entrepreneurial;
- selling;
- traditional/bureaucratic;
- quality.

Each has quite distinct characteristics, as summarised in Table 4.

Entrepreneurial organisations tend to centre on individuals who have strong personal leadership. The culture is almost invariably informal and highly participative; staff are creative and loyal; decision-making is usually focused on a limited range of product/customer segments, and can therefore be responsive and often intuitive. Large companies often create separate divisions or companies to get new products off the ground, encouraging an entrepreneurial style that is deliberately different from the normal company culture.

If entrepreneurial organisations succeed, they tend to evolve into *selling* organisations. Survival depends on an aggressive push for volume and market share; the focus of management attention is on turnover and sales force performance; creativity takes second place to cash flow; formalised procedures begin to take hold.

If the entrepreneurial leader survives the company's evolution to a selling organisation, he or she is seldom able to live with the overwhelming mediocrity of the *bureaucratic* organisation: functional specialism and parochialism start to dominate; internal communications become formal and unresponsive, extending lead times; the focus moves to medium-term cost/benefit. Growth often outstrips management's capacity to understand what is happening in processes that remain cross-functional. Bureaucratic organisations often retreat into niche markets, but carry administrative overheads and practices that limit their capacity to innovate and respond to changing customer needs.

Surviving the bureaucratic organisation means developing a culture that combines responsiveness to customer needs with efficiency, that provides direction and control without stifling innovation, and that is adaptive to changing markets and competitive challenges. This is the *quality* organisation, which is able to develop its internal capability to meet its strategic market positioning.

Table 4 Organisational classification[7]

	Entrepreneurial	Selling	Bureaucratic	Quality
Management style	Personal leadership Visionary Participative	Aggressive Reward driven Directive	Functional or parochial Political Directive Procedure driven	Cooperative Participative Cross-functional Process driven
Culture	Loyal Inspirational Creative Informal	Competitive Fear Divisive Becoming formal	'Efficiency' Fear Protective Formal	Empowering Customer-driven Supportive Team building Informal
Reward system	Erratic	Commission Performance related	Budgetary Length of service	Company/team profit share
Change	Ad Hoc Responsive Opportunity Breakthrough	Limited Reactive	Limited Unresponsive Threat Top-down	Continuous improvement Responsive Opportunity Innovation
Resources	Meagre Flexible	Salesmen	Specialist Functional Wasteful	Flexible Adaptive
Decisions	Intuitive Subjective Qualitative	Quantitative	Cost/benefit Quantitative	Qualitative Quantitative Focused
Control/ measurement	Loose Instinctive Cash flow driven	Focused Market share or sales revenue driven	Budgetary Hierarchical Input (cost) driven	Knowledge Understanding Output (service) driven
Communication	Telling Oral Discussion Open	Telling Oral or written Instruction 'Need to know' Centre outwards	Telling Written Restrictive/ defensive 'Need to know' Functional Tactical	Listening Oral or written Information sharing Open Cross-functional processes Customer-oriented
Horizon	Short term	Short term	Short to medium term	Short/medium/long term
Competitive stance	New Steal	Steal	Defend	New Nurture Steal Defend

Without an understanding of the type of organisation a company has assumed, attempts to bring cohesion and single-mindedness to its operations will probably be piecemeal and ineffective. Contradictory policies, internal politics and vested interests will conspire to limit the continuous change needed to adjust positioning and keep capability in step. Identifying a company's organisational characteristics is not therefore simply an interesting academic exercise: it is essential in identifying the barriers to change so that a strategy for dismantling them can be formulated.

> An engineering company had become strongly 'bureaucratic' in its approach. As it became more and more hidebound by stultifying procedures and standards, overseas competition was growing increasingly innovative in its product developments. Before long, the company was left way behind the market in the features and performance its products offered. It had failed to recognise the positioning it required to meet the demands of a faddish market and the capability needed to respond rapidly to its whims. The company found that simply placing objectives of faster product development on its managers had little effect. It had to make clear to all involved the new positioning it had to adopt and to challenge fundamentally the procedures by which tasks were planned and performed. Only through the organisation's patient but dogged determination did people's approach to their work change and the blindly accepted norms gradually disappear.

Repositioning involves *changing capability*, as the following four examples from different industries illustrate.

1 In the 1960s Toyota manufactured a range of medium-sized saloon cars. Within that product/market segment it developed a capability for high quality at low cost. From the formidable position it developed in that specific base, the company has over the last 30 years continuously improved in order to be able to extend its high quality/low cost capability to the luxury car market: the Lexus competes directly with BMW, Mercedes and Jaguar.

2 Direct Line Insurance was established in 1985 by the Royal Bank of Scotland to market motor insurance in the UK. Its main innovation was direct telephone sales to the public, bypassing conventional sales channels that use intermediaries. It now has a significant and growing share of the UK motor insurance market. Its competitive capability derived from the delivery of outstanding customer service at low cost, both at the point of sale and in the servicing of insurance claims. Behind this lies a formidable operational capability which also delivers comprehensive management information. It

has since extended its capability into house contents insurance – a new product – to the same customer base. Direct Line has an uncompromising attitude to the development of its capability, involving not only the development of its computing and telecommunications systems, but also the development of its people – through training and education in customer needs and, critically, through delegation of responsibility.

3 A bus manufacturer survived a drastic downturn in its business by focusing not only on the needs of its *direct* customers – the fleet operators – but on the needs of the *end consumer*, the fare paying passenger. This involved understanding two sets of needs:

- *passengers'* needs for comfort, easy access, personal safety, information, convenient methods of payment, and low cost;
- *operators'* needs for a low whole-life cost, reliability, ease of maintenance and cleaning, low running costs, and spares availability.

Through understanding these needs, the company developed a clear definition of the product/customer segments in which it could excel. It assessed its competitors' capabilities within those segments against its own, and built manufacturing, marketing, selling and distribution capabilities that would differentiate it in its chosen segments.

4 A pensions and life assurance company selling products through intermediaries recognised that its main contact with customers was reactive: it only talked to them when they complained or made enquiries about their policies. Product design had been the preserve of actuaries – Sales was not involved – and Marketing was left with the task of producing brochures. Development of capability was limited to providing an IT system to process new products. Subsequent poor product performance was blamed on sales force incompetence.

The company's chances of cross-selling to customers was limited by their initial experience of the sale conversion process, a drawn-out saga of quotations, medical examinations, queries, delays, all enmeshed in documents phrased in impenetrable English. The subsequent support process merely reinforced customers' early convictions.

Change was brought about by researching and quantifying customer needs, measuring competitor performance in terms of product features and customer service, and using technology to streamline conversion and support processes. It provided its independent sales force with leads, and indicated where potential customers could be found and what they were likely to buy. The sales force was given a voice in the development of new products; Marketing was given ownership of product launch and life-cycle management. Through these changes both positioning and capability were altered. The effects on sales, customer support and costs were dramatic.

Summary

At senior level, most companies have a pretty good understanding of their positioning with regard to their customers and competitors. Much more frequently, they have only a vague knowledge of their capability to meet their customers' needs, and to determine what has to change and how to bring that change about.

Establishing a company's true capability, linking it to positioning and implementing an action plan for change are the difficult steps. An understanding of corporate capabilities demands not only knowledge but also a culture within which people can openly reveal process shortcomings without fear of personal retribution.

Devising and agreeing steps to change capability to meet a company's positioning requires teamwork and cooperation between managers, and excellent communication throughout the organisation. If this can be achieved, the organisation will have focused the efforts of everyone on meeting efficiently the real needs of the right customers.

CHAPTER 4

Delighting the customer

'It will not suffice to have customers that are merely satisfied. An unhappy customer will switch. Unfortunately, a satisfied customer may also switch, on the theory that he could not lose much, and might gain.'

Dr W. Edwards Deming

In both the public and private sectors, organisations are under pressure to improve customer service and to reduce costs. Those who succeed will be those who best meet the needs of their customers – not meet them more or less, but meet them so well, and so consistently, that their customers are delighted.

Organisations do not possess infinite resources to pour into customer service. They must focus on the most important elements, and they must perform them efficiently. This all sounds wonderfully simple, but those who have been involved in trying to deliver customer service know it isn't so. It requires a good understanding of what the customer really wants, shared by all. However, the key elusive ingredient is an understanding throughout the organisation of everyone's role in supporting the delivery of customer service.

This means cooperation and teamwork.

In this chapter, we discuss the key issues involved in delighting customers, and some pointers as to how this may be achieved.

Good enough or excellent?

We have already said that Total Quality is a system of behaviour. The view that quality relates only to conformance to specification is nowadays too narrow. It is certainly not the view of the *customer*, who probably knows or cares little about whether the product conforms. Customers have a sharper focus, measuring quality against competing products or services, and against their own particular requirements, many of which will not be found in a formal specification, even if one exists.

It is not good enough simply to match the rest. The key to service leadership is *delighting the customer*. Leading companies provide superior service to win customer loyalty and rely on customer recommendations to win greater market share. Loyal customers are the base for business success: they resist competitive attempts to steal market share; they are cheap to supply and they are free, impartial ambassadors to your potential customers.

Do you know what wins the loyalty of your customers? Do you improve the processes of your business to ensure you keep their loyalty? Do you track how well you are doing?

Inferior quality

What becomes of the customers you fail to please? Customer service research[8] has shown that, of every 100 dissatisfied customers:

- only four complain;
- 91 say they will never buy from that supplier again, although 87 *would* remain loyal if only the supplier tried to solve the problem;
- each unhappy customer tells 12 others.

So the danger is that, unless companies take pains to find out what their customers think, they will remain blissfully ignorant of the dissatisfaction they are causing: all they will note is a few complaints and an inexplicable lack of repeat buying.

However, there is worse: where there are displeased customers, there is usually a great deal of internal wasted effort as well. For example, firefighting, checking, clarifying instructions, correcting errors, warranty work and issuing credit notes. We call this wasted effort *diversionary*.

These diversionary activities all contribute to the *cost of poor quality*, which in our experience can represent as much as 40 per cent of sales. Gradual and continuous quality improvement is crucial in cutting out diversionary activities. We refer to cost of poor quality and diversionary activities in detail in Chapter 7.

Improved quality gives rise not to higher, but to lower cost operations, as well as delighted customers. A virtuous circle is created: delighted customers do not need intensive sales efforts, so selling resources can be channelled into increasing market share. At the same time, lower costs allow more product or service development to take place, providing the opportunity of providing yet more delight for customers.

It is tantalising to consider how much more seriously managers would take the issue of service quality if the cost of quality were not so well hidden. Take the fact that only 4 per cent of dissatisfied customers complain. Would managers take more notice if they *all* complained and the customer service department had to be 25 times as big? Would they take note if they knew the selling costs which went into replacing customers who were satisfied but not delighted?

Researching expectations and perceptions

The starting point for any company looking to improve quality is a customer needs survey. It establishes the requirements of both existing and potential customers. It defines the areas in which excellence will be rewarded by winning and delighting those customers. Properly executed, it will establish

Figure 7 *Customer needs survey*

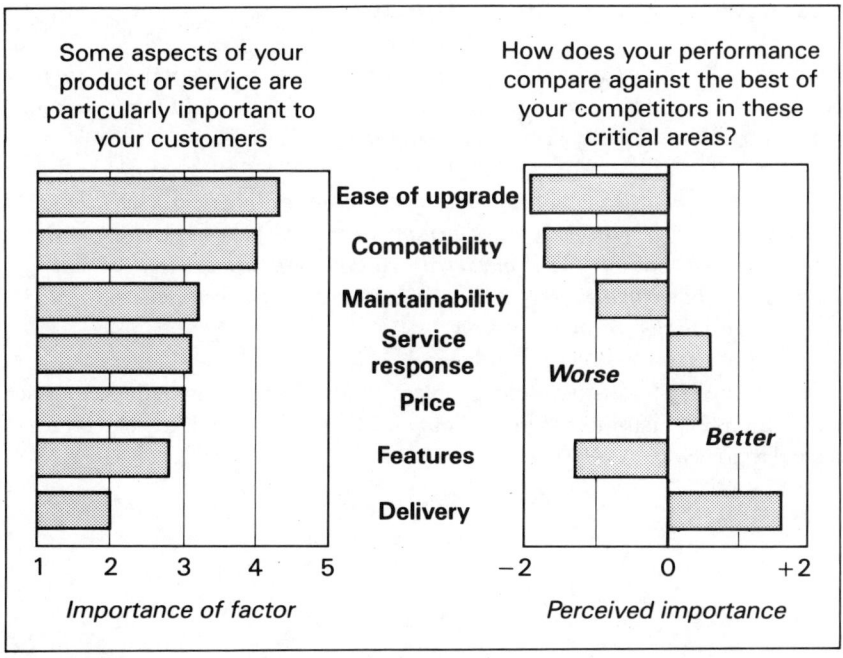

43

how well the company is presently perceived to meet customer needs, and will prompt it to consider alternatives to its present levels of service.

> *A UK electronics company was failing to satisfy the most important needs of its customers: ease of upgrade of equipment, compatibility and maintainability. It was exceeding their expectations in less important areas: service response and delivery. The disadvantage of providing a poor service on what mattered most to the customer far outweighed the benefits of good service on what mattered least.*

Understanding the relative importance of different *aspects* of customer service is critical to winning a competitive edge through superior service.

A customer needs survey will highlight gaps and deficiencies in service and indicate the improvements required to bridge the gap between customers' expectations and perceptions. It may also identify areas where service levels can be reduced at minimal risk in order to re-deploy resources to more important areas.

Perceived versus actual quality

As an added complexity, companies must be prepared to accept that there may be a gap between the service quality they actually deliver and their customers' perception of that quality. You may be in for a nasty shock.

> *A survey conducted for a supplier of office machinery (Figure 8) established that marketing efforts had created a mean expectation of two weeks' lead time from order to delivery. The measured lead time performance averaged four weeks. Unfortunately the delays affected customers' perceptions: they estimated the figure to be five weeks.*

So this supplier had a two-fold problem: not only was his delivery service worse than the customers expected but also they perceived it to be even more dismal than it was!

Figure 8 *Measured service performance*

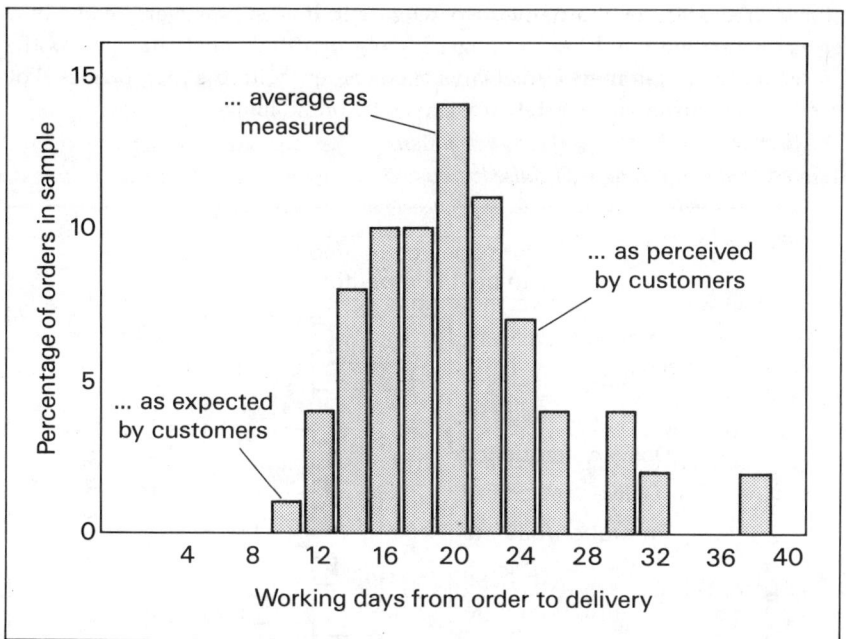

Ten ways to delight your customers

If meeting customers' needs is so important, why is it that companies do it so badly? One reason is that the cost of failure is usually invisible to senior management. But there are many others.

Avoid gaps between customer expectations and management perceptions

Customer expectations and management perceptions of those expectations often differ, sometimes substantially. Take the case of our office equipment supplier. An analysis of customers' and management's ranked service factors (Figure 9) highlighted the differences in perception: the service factor ranked top by management did not even figure in the customer's Top 12!

What hope can suppliers have of delighting customers if they are not even aware of what factors do so?

As a result of following the wrong priorities, the supplier was failing to meet its customers' key needs: fast delivery and good stock availability. Only half of all deliveries met the two-week despatch target. It was, however, excellent in terms of durability and brand image, having invested substantially in both. Unfortunately, customers had always been content with the previous level of durability, and were completely unswayed by brand image.

Figure 9 *Office equipment supplier*

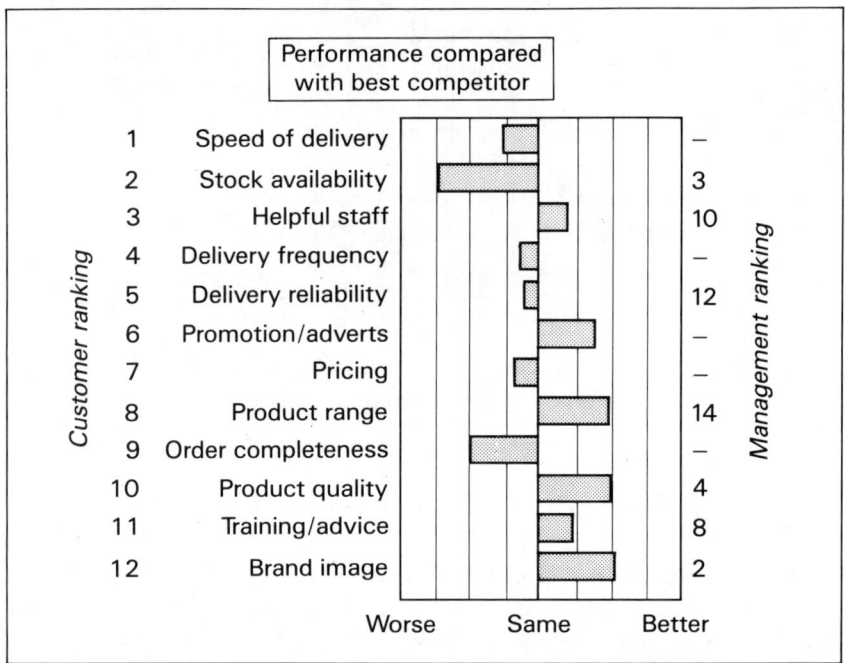

Measure service performance

Companies frequently fail to measure service performance. Without facts, management is denied the means to make rational decisions, and falls back on intuition and emotion. Even when facts are collected, they are often not the ones that will enable managers to improve customer service. Quality of service must be defined in terms the customer values. Internal measures of quality, such as productivity standards and absence of defects are not sufficient and can be positively misleading.

In the case of the office equipment supplier, the computer told management that over 90 per cent of orders were delivered within the company's two week

46

target. But this statistic was based on the *first* delivery, which was frequently a part order. A different analysis showed the true service level in the eyes of the customer: only 53 per cent of orders were *completed* within the target.

The culture of the company was such that managers feared retribution if customer service was found to be poor. So they chose measures which put them in a good light, but which hid the extent of customer dissatisfaction.

Selecting the *correct* performance measures is crucially important. Apart from anything else, measuring and tracking them is time-consuming. If they are inappropriate to meeting customers' needs, this time is wasted. But more importantly, inappropriate measures cause people to work on quite the wrong priorities.

The discipline of measuring and tracking process performance will stimulate people to seek ways to improve it. There is often no need to set goals or targets. However, it is vital to institute a 'feedback' mechanism which enables your staff to resolve quality problems which arise elsewhere in your company, or even with your suppliers, without recrimination or blame.

Improve processes rather than set targets

It is a perceived wisdom that setting targets is a core management activity: the tougher the targets, the better management is doing its job.

When senior managers emphasise corporate targets such as sales, productivity or market share, they often fail to understand that *quality* is the key to achieving them. It is all too easy for managers to set targets which would be wonderful to achieve, but which the processes of the business are incapable of delivering. Staff who work within the processes realise the impossibility of meeting the target and just give up. Alternatively, if the target is easy to achieve, staff will simply slow down and relax.

Given the right organisational culture – or system of behaviour – staff will work as hard as they can to improve customer service *within the constraints of the processes with which they work*. They will do so through a natural desire to do as well as they can. They don't need management to 'motivate' them, exhort them or set them targets: they *do* need management to help them improve the capabilities of the processes. Management must help them measure their own performance, and solve problems. They must also invest in training, systems and procedures.

Put senior management close to customers

In a large organisation, senior management is often remote not only from customers but also from the staff who deal directly with them. Customer contact is restricted to reading reports and summaries – no substitute for dealing with them direct.

Moreover, each layer in the organisation structure filters messages. Like Chinese whispers, information about customers' expectations either does not reach the managers who can act, or it becomes distorted on the way.

In all companies, top managers must experience customers' expectations and perceptions first-hand. They must create opportunities for direct customer contact. They must listen to staff who are a prime source of information on customer perceptions and service delivery problems. Like one Quality Director who made over 100 visits to customers in a year, managers should develop a formal programme of visits – to the work areas within the business and to customers – in order to experience the everyday problems of service delivery.

Make managers commit to quality

The most frequently quoted *root* cause of poor customer service, standing head and shoulders above the rest, is lack of management commitment to quality.

The role of managers in a quality organisation is to help their staff improve the processes in which they work and meet customers' *real* requirements. Such a role demands that managers develop a deep understanding of the processes of the business. They must also possess an ability to interact easily and effectively with those beneath them and with other managers in different parts of the organisation.

Many managers find this role altogether too demanding. Other managers find that the organisational culture prevents them from managing in this way. Most find themselves focusing on arbitrary numerical targets: increase sales by 10 per cent this year; cut costs by 5 per cent the next. Those who succeed are rewarded, those who fail are punished.

Deming claims that only 5 per cent of defects are caused by individual error. The remaining 95 per cent are due to failures in processes, the very processes which *managers* in a Total Quality company ought to be tasked with continuously improving.

Deming has a radical definition of quality. One of his prerequisites is to *'remove the barriers to pride in workmanship'*.

Do *you* permit those who work for you pride in what they do? Or do you force them to take actions which they *know* will dissatisfy the very customers they are trying hard to delight: shipping defective goods in order to meet month-end targets, cutting important customer services to achieve arbitrary profit forecasts?

Managers must be prepared to resist the easy options, the routes to short-term profitability at the expense of long-term survival and growth. They must put delighting the customer before all else, and be seen to do so by everyone within the organisation. They must build the base of loyal customers on which their corporate future depends.

Broken service promises

A TV rental company promised that any customer who telephoned the company's repair centre before 10 am would receive a same day call from an engineer. However, the repair centres were unable to handle the volume of calls, and customers became frustrated trying to get through. Having had their expectations raised by the service promise and then dashed, customers reacted by attributing to the rental company a poorer reputation for service than it had before.

The message to managers is clear: by all means make a service promise, but only when you have satisfied yourself that you have set up processes capable of meeting that promise consistently. Give your people training in what needs doing, employing the right technology for the job, and create robust processes that will deliver the service.

The same message applies to service charters, or citizens' charters: they reposition the organisation, raising customer expectations. Until the internal capability matches the expectation, the charter will be counter-productive.

Don't constrain managers

When a line manager has limited authority to change the way staff work within the processes they operate, he or she is constrained to 'think small', to reject the challenge of improving customer service on the grounds that improvements are not possible.

Yet a commitment to quality demands a constant striving for improvement. Managers must feel secure enough, and have sufficient authority, to challenge the way things are done. They must be allowed to experiment and to modify the approach, in order to deliver improved customer service.

Improve process design

If a service delivery process is poorly designed, employees will fail to meet customer expectations, no matter how hard they try.

By trying hard, and failing, they will become demotivated. To make matters worse, management will probably blame the *employees*, not the *process*, which will demotivate them even more.

There are many causes of poor processes, such as:

- illogical sequencing of steps;
- tasks not standardised;
- conflicting objectives;
- lack of accountability or authority;
- poor documentation;
- insufficient, or poorly trained staff;
- inadequate tools or equipment.

> *A specialist finance company promised its customers it would turn round applications for business loans within 24 hours. Its service delivery process was designed as a series of tasks, each performed by a different specialist group. The process worked effectively when volumes were constant. However, as soon as volume peaked, bottlenecks appeared and the 24-hour response was not delivered to customers. No matter how quickly staff worked, they simply could not get a high volume of applications through every link in the process in time. The main problem was the sequencing of the steps in the process. Each had to be completed before the next step could begin and some types of loan had to loop back to an earlier stage. In front of some sections were piles of loan forms waiting to be processed. Managers redesigned the process so that it consisted of several parallel steps, carried out by a smaller number of larger work groups. This eliminated bottlenecks and enabled employees to meet the company's service delivery goal. As a bonus, it allowed the company to differentiate priority clients and give them an even better service.*

Let employees control processes

To make the concept of improving customer service meaningful, employees must feel they are able to respond flexibly to customer needs. This in turn means they should have the degree of control over the process which is appropriate to their level and their capability. They should not be restricted by having decisions which they are capable of taking forced higher up the organisation than necessary.

Low employee control over the processes they operate jeopardises service quality. It creates delays and disruptions and inhibits people's natural enthusiasm and innovation. Managers should not only put time and effort into designing processes and training their people to meet customer expectations, but they should also encourage employees to react innovatively to customers' needs.

An excellent example is Shelley Berman's famous exchange of letters with a hotel,[9] whose policy of delighting customers included the issuing of free soap to its guests.

'Dear Maid
Please do not leave any more of those little bars of soap in my bathroom since I have brought my own bath-sized Dial. Please remove the six unopened little bars from the shelf under the medicine chest and another three in the shower soap dish. They are in my way. Thank you.
S. Berman

Dear Room 635
I am not your regular maid. She will be back tomorrow, Thursday, from her day off. I took the 3 hotel soaps out of the shower soap dish as you requested. The 6 bars on your shelf I took out of your way and put on top of your Kleenex dispenser in case you should change your mind. This leaves only the 3 bars I left today which are my standing instructions from the management. I hope this is satisfactory.
Kathy, Relief Maid

Dear Maid
I hope you are my regular maid,
Apparently Kathy did not tell you about my note to her concerning the little bars of soap. When I got back to my room this evening I found you had added 3 little Camays to the shelf under my medicine cabinet. I am going to be here in the hotel for two weeks and have brought my own bath-size Dial so I won't need those 6 little Camays which are on the shelf. They are in my way when shaving, brushing teeth, etc. Please remove them.
S. Berman

Dear Mr Berman
My day off was last Wednesday so the relief maid left 3 hotel soaps which we are instructed to do by the management. I took the 6 soaps which were in your way on the shelf and put them in the soap dish where your Dial was. I put the Dial in the medicine cabinet for your convenience. I did not remove the 3 complimentary soaps which are always placed inside the medicine cabinet for all new check-ins and

which you did not object to when you checked in last Monday. Please let me know if I can be of further assistance.
Your regular maid, Dotty

Dear Mr Berman
The assistant manager, Mr Kensedder informed me this morning that you called him last evening and said you were unhappy with your maid service. I have assigned a new girl to your room. I hope you will accept my apologies for any past inconvenience. If you have any future complaints please contact me so I can give it my personal attention. Call extension 1108 between 8 am and 5 pm. Thank you.
Elaine Carmen, Housekeeper

Dear Mrs Carmen
It is impossible to contact you by phone since I leave the hotel for business at 7.45 am and don't get back before 5.30 pm. That's the reason I called Mr Kensedder last night – you were already off duty. I only asked Mr Kensedder if he could do anything about those little bars of soap. The new maid you assigned me must have thought I was a new check-in today, since she left another 3 bars of hotel soap in my medicine cabinet along with her regular delivery of 3 bars on the bathroom shelf. In just 5 days here I have accumulated 24 little bars of soap. Why are you doing this to me?
S. Berman

Der Mr Berman
Your maid, Kathy, has ben instructed to stop delivering soap to your room and remove the extra soaps. If I can be of further assistance, please call extension 1108 between 8.00 am and 5.00 pm. Thank you.
Elaine Carmen, Housekeeper

Dear Mr Kensedder
My bath-size Dial is missing. Every bar of soap was taken from my room including my own bath-size Dial. I came in late last night and had to call the bellhop to bring me 4 little Cashmere Bouquets.
S. Berman

Dear Mr Berman
I have informed our housekeeper, Elaine Carmen, of your soap problem. I cannot understand why there was no soap in your room since our maids are instructed to leave 3 bars of soap each time they

service a room. The situation will be rectified immediately. Please accept my apologies for the inconvenience.
Martin K. Kensedder, Asst. Manager

Dear Mrs Carmen
Who the hell left 54 little bars of Camay in my room? I came in last night and found 54 little bars of soap. I don't want 54 little bars of Camay. I want my one damn bar of bath-size Dial. Do you realise I have 54 bars of soap in here. All I want is my bath-size Dial. Please give me back my bath-size Dial.
S. Berman

Dear Mr Berman
You complained of too much soap in your room so I had them removed. Then you complained to Mr Kensedder that all your soap was missing so I personally returned them – the 24 Camays which had been taken and the 3 Camays you are supposed to receive daily. I don't know anything about the 4 Cashmere Bouquets. Obviously your maid, Kathy, did not know I had returned your soaps so she also brought 24 Camays plus the 3 daily Camays. I don't know where you got the idea this hotel issues bath-size Dial. I was able to locate some bath-size Ivory which I will leave in your room.
Elaine Carmen, Housekeeper

Dear Mrs Carmen
Just a short note to bring you up-to-date on my latest soap inventory.
   As of today I possess:
On shelf under medicine cabinet – 18 Camay in 4 stacks of 4 and 1 stack of 2.
On Kleenex dispenser – 11 Camay in 2 stacks of 4 and 1 stack of 3.
On bedroom dresser – 7 Cashmere Bouquet in 1 stack of 3 and 1 stack of 4, 1 hotel-size bath-size Ivory, and 8 Camay in 2 stacks of 4.
Inside medicine cabinet – 14 Camay in 3 stacks of 4 and 1 stack of 2.
In shower soap dish – 6 Camay, very moist.
On northeast corner of tub – 1 Cashmere Bouquet, slightly used.
On northwest corner of tub – 6 Camays in 2 stacks of 3.

Please ask Kathy when she services my room to make sure the stacks are neatly piled and dusted. Also, please advise her that stacks of more than 4 have a tendency to tip. May I suggest that my bedroom window sill, which is not in use, will make an excellent spot for future soap deliveries. One more item, I have purchased another bar of

bath-size Dial which I am keeping in the hotel vault in order to avoid
further misunderstandings.
S. Berman'

Such humour works because it is so uncomfortably close to reality! Note the
true to life reaction of the housekeeper to the customer's initial complaint to the
Assistant Manager about the soap delivery process: replace the maid. No
wonder staff in some organisations carry out management instructions to the
letter, however bizarre those instructions may appear to be.

It is worth recalling the statistic at the beginning of this chapter that each
unhappy customer tells 12 others.

Encourage teamwork

From the customer's point of view, a large part of the organisation providing a
service remains hidden. The customer has contact only with certain staff – the
sales person, the delivery driver, the telephonist. Yet behind these are many
more who, if things go according to plan, should remain invisible to the
customer – sales administration staff who process the order, production
planners who set up the production run and so on.

Each of these invisible people forms a vital link in the process chain which
allows the customer contact staff finally to deliver the required service to the
customer. If one link in the chain breaks – for example, if a sales invoice is
incorrect or if production materials run out – service to the customer is at risk.

It is easy to fall into the trap of targeting service improvement on contact
employees alone. This underestimates the effect that poor quality in the
internal customer/supplier chain can have on the quality of service as
perceived by the external customer.

Breaks in the chain are most likely to happen when there is a lack of
teamwork among the people who form the process chain; when departmental
barriers are high, and people do not fully understand the interdependencies in
the process.

This is where the concept of internal customers plays its part. Delivering
service to the external customer involves internal customers and suppliers in a
chain of service relationships: each internal customer has service requirements
which each internal supplier has to meet.

The first step is for internal suppliers to find out exactly what their customer
– in this case the internal customer – wants.

This sounds simple but is often deceptively so. In practice, it requires a
culture in which departmental barriers are broken down and where internal

suppliers actively seek the views of their customers in order to improve service. Internal customers provide constructive criticism in an atmosphere free from blame and recrimination. They quantify the levels of service they need from their suppliers in order to meet the needs of their *own* customers.

Summary

In the 1990s, the successful companies will be those determined to achieve the highest standards of customer service – by constantly monitoring, and where possible anticipating, customers' expectations and perceptions.

The foundation for service leadership is a strategy for delighting the customer. It entails:

- an unequivocal commitment to quality by top management;
- a willingness to go to extraordinary lengths to ensure that new products and services meet customers' expectations;
- a willingness to be self-critical and to ask customers – internal and external – to comment on performance;
- an analytical approach to improving continuously every aspect of service delivery and product/service quality.

The culture of the organisation must be open and receptive to the principles underlying excellence in service provision. Service quality cannot flourish if the culture is tainted by:

- fear of recrimination if process failures are brought to light;
- hierarchical barriers between management and staff;
- inter-departmental barriers between groups who *should* be working in close cooperation.

The fundamental goal of Total Quality is to have delighted customers. The barriers are usually cultural.

CHAPTER 5

The role of management

'We are going to win and the industrial West is going to lose out: there's nothing much you can do about it, because the reasons for failure are within yourself . . . for you, the essence of management is getting the ideas out of the heads of the bosses into the hands of labour . . . for us, the core of management is precisely the act of mobilising and pulling together the intellectual resources of all employees . . . only by drawing on the combined brainpower of all its employees can a firm face up to the turbulence and constraints of today's environment.'

Konosuke Matsushita

We have defined Total Quality as a system of behaviour. This definition commits one to a never-ending task: in a dynamic world, customer needs continuously change, not least because we raise their expectations whenever we deliver quality products and services; and opportunities to lower costs, even if only through technological advances, arise unceasingly.

What's wrong with Western management practice?

The key problem is management by results. This system of management emphasises a chain of command, and a hierarchy of objectives, systems and decision-making. Results are enshrined in numerical quotas and standards that bear little relation to the capability of the process in which people are working. Focus on the end results, rather than on the systems and processes that deliver them, corrupts the processes themselves.

A life assurance company set a target of two days for the processing of new business. The target was rigorously enforced by management because it was perceived to offer a competitive advantage in the market place. The problem was that volumes of new business were not consistent. At peak times, the staff could not properly meet the target. The only way the standard could then be met was by working less diligently, which meant that inconsistencies and errors on customers applications went undetected until a later stage in a different department. Although one department met its targets, doing so forced another into unnecessary activity, and prevented it meeting its own performance standard.

The managing director of a manufacturing company insisted that all calls to the switchboard should be answered within ten seconds. He monitored the statistics personally. Switchboard operators resorted to putting callers abruptly through to the Personnel Department if they showed signs of needing help.

Checkout operators in a supermarket were measured on the rate at which objects were scanned through the checkout. They therefore preferred to leave the customers buried in products as they struggled to pack them at the same rate, rather than to stop scanning and help.

The use of such arbitrary numerical targets fosters a number of problems:

- It encourages short-term thinking, even at the expense of medium- or long-term objectives that may be essential to corporate survival.
- Functional targets are emphasised at the expense of other functions, creating a climate of distrust and internal conflict.
- Individual targets are met at the expense of other people in the team, creating peer competition and destroying team work.
- They create fear. People are frightened of the consequences, even though they tried their best. Fear is the prime motivator in a management by results system.
- They encourage inward thinking rather than the external focus required to meet customer requirements.

Whatever numbers are used, they often fail to reflect reality because staff learn to fudge the figures, making them meaningless. Management, reading the indicators, believes that the organisation is performing as expected, but is blind to what is really happening.

The first comprehensive survey into the experiences of British Businesses of 'Quality Improvement' initiatives[10] revealed that many UK companies have responded to the threat of increasing competition and the flood of imports by

Figure 10 Initiatives undertaken by British business

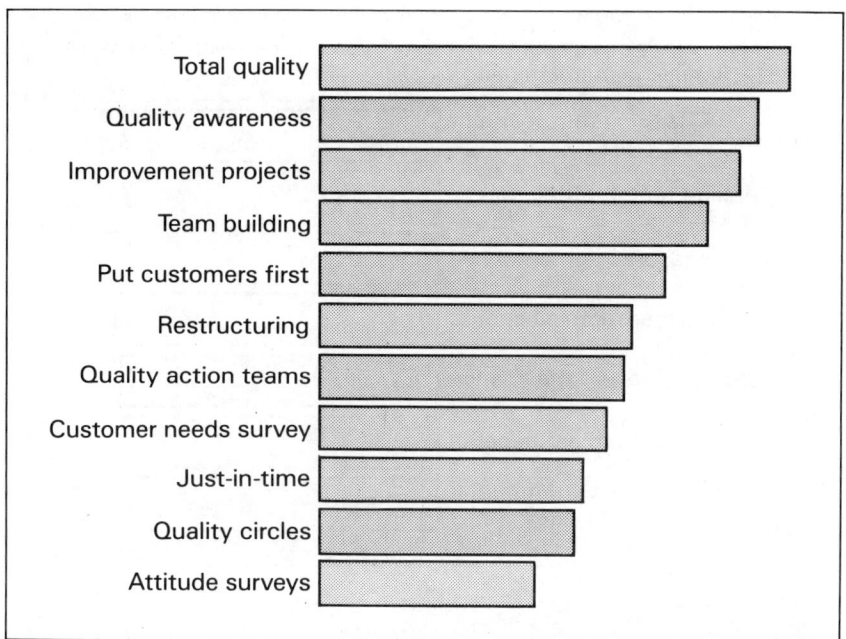

initiating a variety of quality improvement programmes. By far the most popular among these was Total Quality (Figure 10).

However, while the awareness of Total Quality is high, the average level of improvement, in particular the key measure of profitability, is depressingly low. The main reasons are shown in Figure 11.

The problems that companies face fall into two categories. The first is concerned with *the way Total Quality is initiated*. This includes not being able to understand the process of change, and to find the time to manage it; inability to measure the results – which implies that measurement was not used in generating the need for change – and therefore failure to obtain tangible benefits; extended timescales and lost momentum; and poor internal communications.

The second and more significant category of problems is concerned with *management behaviour*. This involves the difficult question of culture change, and the role of management in providing the necessary leadership. The most powerful barriers to change are invariably the accepted norms of behaviour that in the past have constituted models of success.

Figure 11 *Barriers to Quality improvement*

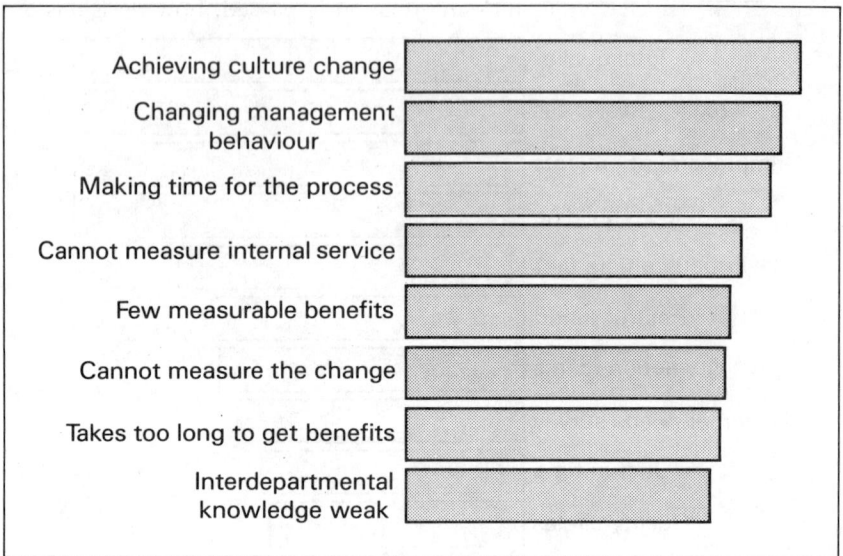

There is a style of management that is much admired throughout British industry – that of the decisive manager. Bring the decisive manager a problem, and within minutes he will assess it against his own wealth of personal experience, prejudice, intuition and gut feel, and immediately issue instructions to 'solve' the problem – an approach which invariably addresses the symptoms, not the disease. This avoids the 'very difficult bit', which is actually having to find out what is happening in the cross-functional process that has developed a symptom of malaise. We shall develop this medical analogy further.

The meaning of culture

What is the culture of a business? It can be defined as the influence on its employees of its cumulative development since its formation. Sharing of beliefs and values cultivates a common management style. The business develops a way in which knowledge is obtained, analysed and interpreted, a way in which issues are discussed and decisions taken. The culture creates clear limits to its managers' authority.

Management behaviour is therefore prescribed by the culture of the organisation, which defines how information is passed, how decisions are made and who has authority to act.

The two most important barriers to Total Quality, *achieving cultural change* and *changing management behaviour* are therefore two aspects of the same impediment.

But why should the culture of a company and its management's behaviour be such an influence on its ability to adopt Total Quality successfully? To answer this question, we must look at *business processes*.

Business processes

Improving the effectiveness of cross-functional business processes requires communication and cooperation across functional boundaries. The problems that managers experience in communicating with their colleagues is illustrated by the results of a staff opinion survey in a large financial service company.

Figure 12 *Problems communicating*

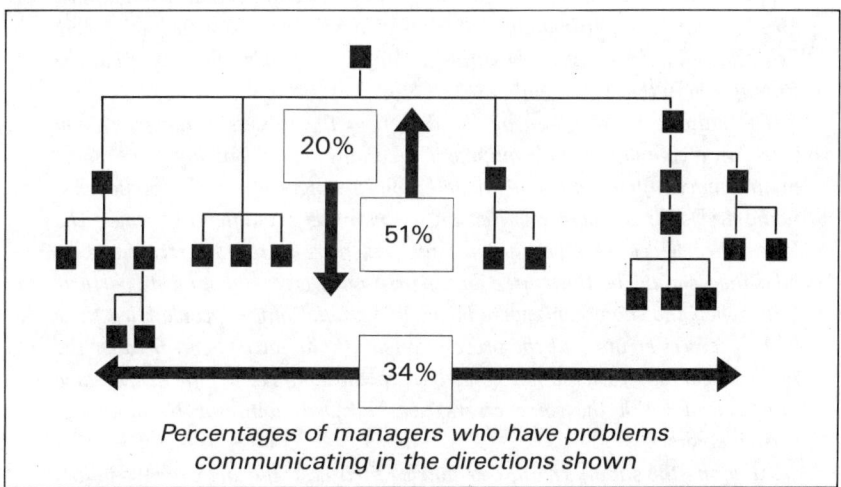

Percentages of managers who have problems communicating in the directions shown

A third of managers felt blocked in talking to their peers in different parts of the organisation. Enlisting the help of their superiors was no help: over half of these self-same managers had problems communicating upwards.

'Viruses'

Process failures are analogous to the effect of viruses. Just as viruses occupy living cells that lack immunity to them, increasing rapidly and transmitting infection, so do viruses live and multiply in weak business processes. They spread throughout the process, infecting other parts of the organisation and diverting them into wasted effort: chasing parts or information; correcting errors; checking work already done; raising credit notes; apologising to customers.

> *A countrywide white goods chain found that 30 per cent of the documents generated in its high street showrooms contained significant errors. The virus spread to regional centres, where staff were responsible for stock-holding and installation. Some documents contained incorrect customer information causing wasted journeys to install equipment. Others contained incorrect stock codes, delaying delivery to the customer.*
>
> *The virus infected head office, where the customers' accounts were maintained, and where the marketing department needed correct coding to maintain a marketing database.*
>
> *The virus was causing people to take corrective action at every point in the supply chain to the customer – wasted effort to the business that cost it almost £5 million a year. Ultimately, the virus also infected customers, who were exposed to the failure of the business to supply the goods they ordered at the time agreed in the showroom.*
>
> *The failures were caused by the design of the process – not by sloppy work. In a complex sale of equipment involving loan financing, insurance, maintenance agreement and installation arrangements, the customers' name and address were required on as many as six different forms. The forms themselves were poorly laid out, and there were no instructions on how they should be filled in. Not surprisingly, errors abounded, particularly when the showrooms were busy. In regional offices people tried their best to correct errors, but the process constantly defeated them. Because the regional computers were not connected to those at Head Office, the same information (with the same errors) was rekeyed, with the possibility of further errors.*
>
> *All along the supply chain, people tried their best, but the* process *failed. Line management had become accustomed to the problems, fought fires, and made whatever improvements they felt able to make within their own sphere of influence. But little changed.*

Total Quality can therefore be seen in terms of *improving business processes*, making them robust so they are immune to the attack of viruses, and ensuring that the needs of the customers – internal or external – at each stage of the process are met.

However, the difficulties of improving business processes can be acute. Staff, through experience, have a good knowledge of their own functional *procedures*, but lack visibility of the overall business *processes*. Even with insight they still lack the authority to make changes: only management can do that. As they rise through the management hierarchy, their perspective broadens together with their authority to introduce change. Unfortunately, making the *right* process changes demands detailed knowledge. As they climb the management ladder, their detailed knowledge weakens. Ultimately, only the board is authorised to change multi-functional processes, but few board members have the knowledge to do so.

Figure 13 *The knowledge/authority gap*

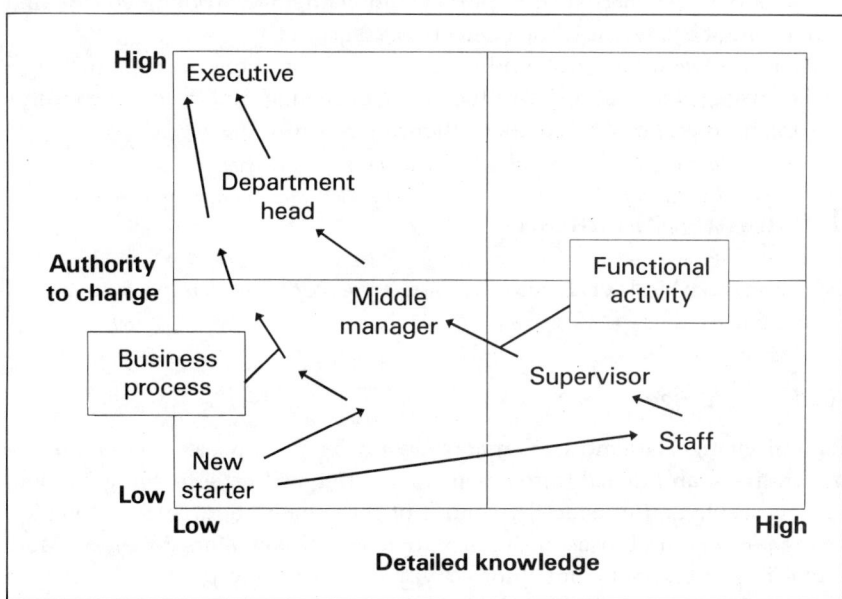

Because processes are multi-functional it is important that communication and cooperation across the organisation is high. However, the business culture may actively discourage cross-functional awareness. The level of understanding can become so low that it is virtually impossible to diagnose the virus or its symptoms. As the problems of communicating between functions increase, the chances of understanding and resolving the problems fall.

Even worse than management's functional parochialism can be its attitude towards staff. Managers often treat staff as if they were incapable of thought. This attitude quickly isolates managers from the very people who have the most knowledge of the process and its failings. Ideas for change from staff are treated with disdain. Managers believe it is *their* role alone to come up with the ideas, and resent others doing so.

But managers, with their lack of detailed understanding of the process, remain unaware of its shortcomings and the diversionary activity it causes. So we have an impasse: management has the authority to improve the process but is blind to the issues. Staff have the knowledge of the issues but are unable to authorise change.

This bitter irony forms an important part of the reason that British businesses in the survey ascribed such importance to changing corporate culture and management behaviour if Total Quality is to succeed.

There are two other, profoundly significant implications of the knowledge/authority gap. The first concerns the nature of change, and the other concerns the organisation's systems of motivation and reward.

The nature of change

There are three kinds of change: radical change, continuous improvement and innovation.

Radical change

Radical change is almost invariably driven by an unwelcome commercial imperative – an *external* factor. Sometimes, this will be something sudden, unforeseeable and outside the control of the organisation, such as political change or a natural disaster that destroys or radically alters a market. More often, it is successful competitor activity or other more progressive change (such as deregulation) that results in declining market share or profitability. In these cases, although the source of the pain is perceived to be external, it usually results from failure to recognise the impending threat and to improve internal competitiveness to meet it. (A vivid illustration of the ability of Japanese industry to plan for, and respond to external threat, is that in the five years to 1987, Japan increased its corporate profitability by 30 per cent, and its annual trade surplus rose from $45 billion to $100 billion, despite its currency rising between 50 per cent and 100 per cent against all major currencies.)

Radical change is always imposed by management, top-down.

Continuous improvement

The second kind of change is continuous improvement. In the absence of continuous improvement, an organisation will decline, even if that decline is only relative to the competition. Most continuous improvement is bottom-up, based on knowledge.

Innovation

The third is innovation. Both innovation and continuous improvement come from within, and can only flourish in a culture that encourages them. If there is a barrier of mistrust between those who have authority (the management) and those who have knowledge (the staff), such a climate cannot exist.

Systems of motivation and reward

An organisation's systems of motivation and reward are broader than pay. 'What is measured, gets done'. We have already observed that an individual is more powerfully influenced by his or her manager's expectations than by what the customer expects. Management expectations and behaviour are driven by many factors – ranging from personal rivalry to the requirement 'to meet budget'. Such factors not only block change, they also cause effort to be misdirected.

In most organisations, financial results are seen as the ultimate measure of performance. This leads to the assumption that the only important measures are financial. This is ironic, since accountants would be the first to admit that, as *management information*, the P&L and the balance sheet leave much to be desired.

We will argue, heretically, that costs and income are secondary. In the same way that income is the *consequence* of delivering a product or service, costs are the *consequence* of decisions to acquire resources – people, equipment, premises, raw material, consumables, and so forth. It is the decisions that need to be better informed. Information on the consequences is secondary.

Managers are of course capable of making bad decisions even when they have good information, but this is no argument for providing misleading or irrelevant information. If the system fails to provide relevant information, that is, it *omits* what is critical or useful, managers are obliged to rely on emotion, prejudice and gut feeling.

Conventional management accounts suffer from a fundamental weakness as management information. Management accounts typically aim to provide managers of cost (and/or profit) centres with a statement of the costs and income for which they are 'accountable'. Every manager receives a sort of mini-P&L. Departments and functions are not separate businesses, but part of the same one. A departmental or functional head can seldom be held fully accountable for the costs that appear in his or her management accounts, since costs are driven cross-functionally. It is therefore important to be clear about what is meant by accountability: for example, we need to distinguish between *method* accountability, which is vertical, and *process* accountability, which is horizontal. A departmental manager normally has method accountability – that is, control over *how* the work is undertaken, but limited or no control over the volumes and service levels being demanded: these are dictated by the needs of internal or external customers. Both method and process account-ability are needed to achieve *total* cost accountability. It requires internal cooperation supported by useful information about customer needs, volumes, capacity, resources, activities, outputs, service levels, and variation. It does *not* mean cross-charging, which never contains this type of information.

By recording only the *costs* (that is, the financial consequence) of input, and sometimes the *income* (the financial consequence) from related outputs, management accounts are rather like parentheses: it's the 'bit between the brackets' that matters.

It is not only 'the bit between the brackets' for each department or function that matters – it affects the whole enterprise. Improvements in the perform-ance of a business are directly related to its ability to improve its cross-functional processes. Management information must therefore provide an informed basis for cross-functional dialogue and cooperation. It must:

- measure outputs and service levels being provided to the customer, internal or external – as an indicator of the effectiveness of the linked activities that generated those outputs;
- embody, reflect and support development of the business strategy, which concerns resource allocation, product and customer mix decisions, and so forth;
- identify whether or not activities add value (are they core, support or diversionary?);
- help, indicate or identify the root cause of process failure and diversionary activity – by tracking back through linked activities;

- help managers to understand capacity – where there is excess capacity and where there are bottlenecks.

One cannot manage costs *directly*. A cost is the *result* of a resource decision – either the decision to acquire the resource in the first place (which cannot usually be 'unacquired' at short notice), or a decision on how that resource should best be used. Because our culture is results-oriented, so are our conventional systems of management information. They focus on the financial consequences, rather than on the means, conditions and circumstances that produce them.

Management of cause and effect is at the heart of sound decisions and commercial success, in an increasingly complex world. Understanding activities and business processes provides the missing link. It is missing from conventional financial and management accounts, and often misleading in conventional standard costing systems.

The accounts function plays a pivotal role in determining what is measured. Accountants are also *managers*, and are in a unique position – by virtue of their professional competence and access to information – to play a vital role in helping management understand such cause and effect.

In Chapter 6 we examine in more detail the barriers to continuous improvement and innovation. Most barriers originate in an organisation's systems of motivation and incentive, in which financial measures play a leading part.

The cure

Managers must free the victims if Total Quality is to succeed. They must empower others to initiate change, and gain knowledge in order to initiate it themselves. Intuition and emotion are a poor basis for success.

Management must decide what it believes the company needs to do to be successful and establish performance measures to check if it is achieving its objectives. It must undertake surveys to determine customer needs and ask customers to assess the company's performance both in absolute terms, and in relation to the competition.

It must participate in bringing together people representing the different parts of the organisation involved in a process. In a structured way, they can then determine how to improve the process by understanding much more clearly the internal customer needs at each stage and the problems that are caused when these needs are not met.

And, with the help of staff – the victims – management must identify and quantify the results of failures so that ideas for change will be focused on identifying root causes and finding best solutions.

The role of the manager

What does 'managing a department' actually mean? Ask most managers what they do and they'll probably reply by giving their job title. But within Total Quality, a manager has a clearly defined role, one that cannot be fulfilled by any other member of staff.

The old role

In an ideal business, the objective is for staff to undertake tasks in robust processes. No diversionary activities would be taking place, and all the core and support activities would be carried out in the most cost-effective manner. External factors affecting the business would generate the need to change the internal processes (see Chapter 3, 'Positioning and capability'). Measuring and gauging these effects form another process. Giving the business its overall strategy and direction form yet another.

As most businesses are far from this ideal, managers have to act on situations that reflect the extent to which the business deviates from the ideal. In addressing these situations, conventional management style displays a number of common characteristics. These are:

- an expectation that quick decisions are a measure of successful management;
- lack of understanding of variation in current processes;
- failure to cooperate across functional boundaries;
- firefighting (dealing with symptoms), rather than searching for root causes of problems;
- a widely held view of subordinates as individuals who make mistakes, rather than as victims of processes that lack robustness;
- appraisal systems that reward individual performance, rather than share the rewards of improved business performance resulting from everyone's contribution to a team effort;
- a reluctance by staff to propose process improvements or highlight what appears to be their own failure in a poor process (the fear factor);
- a reluctance by staff to communicate across functional boundaries at their

own level, if parochial constraints are in evidence at a higher level (the fear factor again).

Over long periods of time these behaviour patterns become the accepted norm for managers. Subordinates take this behaviour as a role model and the pattern is perpetuated. In all companies elements of the pattern will be found to varying degrees.

The new role

In simple terms, the new role will be the opposite of the pattern described above. However, it will not be easy. Few things go seriously wrong in the short term, and because it is difficult to gauge how much better things could be, there is little apparent incentive to change. Such comfort creates considerable inertia against change.

The role of the manager – any manager, in any business – is clear. It is to work continuously on improving business processes, by:

- involving the people that work in the processes (the victims), because they have greater knowledge of the detail;
- cooperating across functional boundaries to improve the effectiveness of the whole process;
- understanding process performance through measurement;
- eliminating fear.

This simple specification is beguiling. The new role requires a cultural change on the manager's part. He or she must be prepared to work *with* staff, using their detailed knowledge and their innate reasoning powers to help management improve the process in which they work. Staff will be surprised, possibly suspicious and certainly curious. A manager will be visibly alone if the current culture is against change. For many managers, the change required provides the moment of truth.

Management has the authority to change processes but it must also be prepared to devolve that authority to staff at a lower level. Doing this is not an act of blind faith: it shows trust in the Total Quality ideal of other peoples' ability to wield authority responsibly. At present, managers spend too much of their time managing diversions and not enough time improving processes.

People watch their managers carefully to see what they do and what they say. Managers are rarely aware of this scrutiny. If they fail to behave as a role model for the way in which they expect their staff to behave, there is little chance of others changing their behaviour.

Figure 14 *Managers' changing use of time*

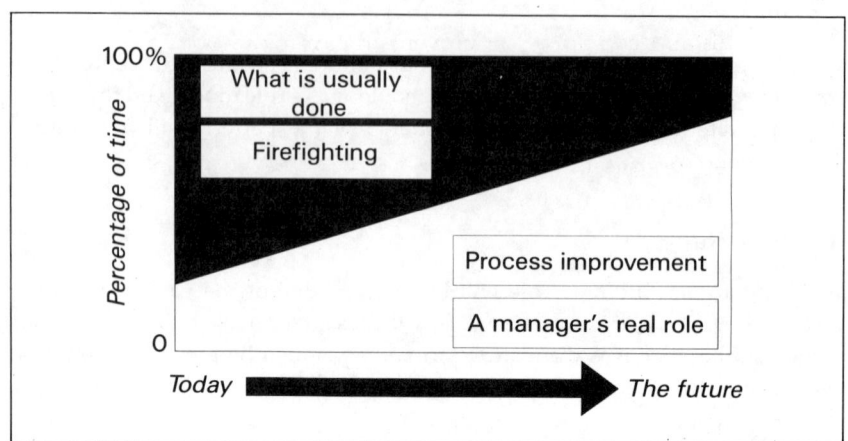

The following is a useful summary of the most important characteristics and behaviour patterns in the new role.[11] Total Quality managers:

- understand the foundations of continuous improvement and their implications for personal behaviour; are consistent in their application; are aware of possible conflicts between their actions and words, and the effects of the kinds of behaviour they condone;
- encourage and support their people to reach the same level of understanding;
- train their people to develop their capability; maintain discipline and ensure adherence to procedures and standards, and are intolerant of sloppy work;
- help their people to understand company and functional direction and priorities;
- are both result and process-oriented;
- use continuous improvement tools and techniques routinely and are disinclined to use emotion or intuition in decision-making;
- actively cooperate with their internal suppliers and customers to improve process quality;
- are aware of external customer requirements and perceptions;
- are never satisfied with the status quo; challenge assumptions and current practice and encourage similar behaviour from their people;
- are fair, open and honest in providing feedback on individual performance, and are highly receptive to receiving feedback from their teams;

- ensure that all their people are actively involved and participate within the team;
- accept mistakes as a price of improvement – avoid censure;
- pay particular attention to communication, especially downwards; ensure that communication is understood, not simply passed down, and that it involves listening and positive response to what they hear;
- practice continual self-improvement;
- use recognition effectively as a means of motivation.

Empowerment

Empowerment is the consequence of changing the role and behaviour of management. You cannot simply tell people they are empowered. You can only create an environment where people feel empowered. An empowered organisation uses all the talents of its people.

Empowerment is prevented by jobs with little perceived meaning, lack of feedback on personal and team performance, lack of guidance of what quality of output is required, rigid job definitions that allow little flexibility or exercise of initiative, constant work pressure, lack of communication, uncaring attitudes, and lack of listening. Most of these problem areas are a reflection of the relationship between managers and their people.

Empowered people feel part of a team, responsible not only for their own results but also for the results of the team. They take pride in what they do, are supported in developing their own full potential, are able to use their initiative, and feel able *to make a difference.*

Empowerment takes time, because managers need to learn that to empower does not lead to loss of control. Instead of looking to managers for direction and control, these are shared with the team. Instead of competing with each other, teams cooperate and count on each other to get a job done. Instead of maintaining discipline by reward and penalty, the manager's role is to support, encourage and stimulate the efforts of his or her team.

We do not pretend that the transition to an empowered organisation is easy. Things will not alter overnight, and some managers will not be capable of change. The greater the degree to which Total Quality challenges the existing business culture, the greater will be management resistance. Most managers will say they are committed to change, but they will remain sceptical of its benefits.

However, managers are as frustrated as their staff after a whole day's diversionary activity. They soon realise that, in their new role, they'll be helped by their staff – and they will become much more effective.

British industry[12] has signalled that a lasting change in corporate culture and in management behaviour are the keys to a successful implementation of Total Quality – and the biggest obstacles. Change in behaviour has to be demonstrated: it cannot just be a strongly articulated commitment. Before setting out on the Total Quality trail, someone has to tell managers just what their jobs are.

And what of the victims themselves, the staff who work in the processes? In a Total Quality company, life for them is transformed. No longer are they expected to do only as instructed, even when their intimate knowledge of the processes in which they work suggests better ways of doing things. They will be encouraged to participate in making improvements – to their working lives and to the company's operations.

Most importantly, they will be accorded respect for their ability to think, challenge and innovate and they will be given recognition for the successes they achieve. Meeting these basic human needs will touch the most cynical and obstinate of working hearts. It will unleash the real potential that gives Total Quality its strength: the genuine enthusiasm of all employees to work together to improve the processes of the business.

One of the corporate value statements of a leading semiconductor manufac turer perfectly describes how we view empowerment:

'If something needs to be done, assume that you have the authority to act. Our responsibility as managers is to support your decisions – not to make them for you.'

CHAPTER 6

Barriers to Total Quality

'Floggings will continue until motivation improves'.

Humorous poster

One of the most common objections to Total Quality is that it works well in the Japanese culture because people are culturally more willing to sacrifice their individual interests for the good of the whole organisation. In the West, individuality is regarded in many quarters as a cultural asset, which is threatened by conformity.

In the first place, the implied facts are highly questionable. It is possible to see British society as highly conformist – for example, in the existence of terms like 'the Establishment' – and not necessarily in a positive way. More to the point, much of our management and industrial relations practice is aimed at conformity – at *removing* discretion from people's activities.

The argument confuses conformity with cooperation and teamwork. Cooperation and teamwork cannot be said to conflict with the interests of the individual, or to leave no room for individuality of thought or action. Indeed, we find it more credible to argue that if attitude to conformity distinguishes Japanese and Western cultures, then the West has an advantage.

The issue is trust. Much restrictive management practice is born of bad experiences of allowing people to exercise discretion. Give them an inch, and they'll take a mile. This flies in the face of common experience, which always contradicts the theory that people are *naturally* untrustworthy, thoughtless, and selfish. In most aspects of people's lives, there is greater self-interest and reward in behaving otherwise.

The barriers to Total Quality are therefore to be found in the nature of change, in organisation structures, and in mechanisms for motivation and reward – whatever form they take.

The nature of change

In Chapter 5, we discussed the role of management, and described the 'knowledge/authority' gap that exists in all but the smallest company.

If managers, and senior managers in particular, lack detailed knowledge of what is happening in business processes, *any change they introduce must therefore be based on ignorance of the detail.* For this reason, top-down change is often radical in nature, unencumbered by the facts. (Someone once suggested that this is not necessarily a bad thing, on the grounds that too much knowledge inhibits flair.)

Furthermore, the requirement is not that senior managers should acquire the same detailed knowledge as their staff, because they have a different job. Along with seniority should come a broader, strategic perspective, and the obligation to make decisions with longer time horizons.

By contrast, bottom-up change is mostly incremental. Staff will suggest changes that are small improvements to the way things are done day to day. This is the essence of continuous improvement.

Much radical, top-down change is initiated because fear and other constraints create a culture in which staff do not feel empowered to propose incremental changes. Without continuous improvement, the effectiveness of the organisation declines to the point where top-down radical change becomes imperative. In these circumstances, it is often also brutal.

Figure 15 *Different approaches to change*

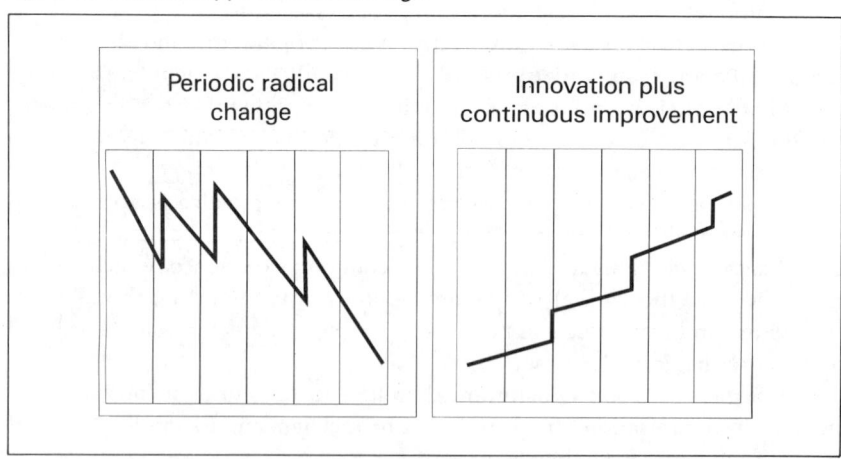

In an environment where continuous improvement is the norm, radical change can originate from any level in the organisation, but it is better described as *innovation*. Figure 15 shows the contrast between an organisation that combines continuous improvement with innovation, and one which is forced to rely on periodic radical change; in the absence of continuous improvement, long-term decline is inevitable, if only in relation to the competition.

Proof of employees' capability to generate both incremental change and innovation comes from a survey comparing the results of Japanese and American suggestion schemes. In Japan, management concentrate on participation and implementation, rather than the quality and value of ideas. The Japanese system (Kaizen – see Chapter 1) involves all employees in making improvements. Their ideas tend to be small scale, inexpensive to implement and concern the individual's own area of work. The results are nevertheless dramatic, shown in Table 5.

Table 5 *Comparison of Japanese and American suggestion schemes*[13]

	USA	Japan (Private organisations only)
Total number of eligible employees	8,364,865	1,685,412
Total number of suggestions received	1,010,889	52,898,345
Number of suggestions per 100 eligible	13	3,145
Percentage of employees participating	9	80
Adoption rate	28.0%	82.5%
Average award payment per adoption	$545.68	$2.70
Average net savings per adoption	$7,663	$43
Net savings per 100 eligible	$26,870	$356,531

The case for empowering staff to suggest change is overwhelming. Our own experience in facilitating bottom-up change in British companies provides indisputable evidence of their capacity and motivation to make proposals for beneficial change.

In a financial services company, the suggestion scheme had generated 48 suggestions in the previous 12 months, of which four had been implemented. As part of the initial adjustment (see Chapter 7) phase of Total Quality, 400 staff generated more than 5,000 ideas in 6 weeks – an average of 1,250 suggestions per 100 eligible staff. More than 3,000 were implemented, with measurable net savings of £600,000 a year. Of these, 9 per cent were regarded as sufficiently radical to need board approval.

Organisation structures

Most management structures are hierarchies that have evolved over many years, gathering layers for a variety of reasons. The rationale usually given for levels of management is the need for appropriate 'spans of control'.

Accepting temporarily (for we will reject the notion later) that there is such a thing as an appropriate span of control, we also find that there are other reasons for levels of management in an organisation.

One is historical pay restraint imposed by government. Promotion became one of the few mechanisms by which it was possible to pay people more.

Another is job evaluation, still extremely popular in large organisations and usually implemented using structured job-scoring methodologies. Such systems are meant to provide a rational management structure based on job content and responsibility, independent of pay. There are few companies that do not use them as methods of controlling pay. Once established, these systems have a robust bureaucracy designed to resist change: allowing any flexibility of operation threatens to upset both applecarts – job structures and salaries.

A job evaluation system requires job descriptions or specifications. When linked to pay systems, a job specification is less an enabling device than a defence mechanism. Any changes to a job description raise the potential for regrading, and therefore higher pay. The system makes such change challenging in order to avoid precedent and creeping escalation. Managers tend to see the job evaluation system as a battleground.

The effect is to set the management structure, and the jobs within it, in organisational concrete. This is the opposite of the flexibility and continuous change needed in a Total Quality organisation. Later on in this chapter, we argue that pay should be related to skills and capability. A management hierarchy may be appropriate at the time it is devised, but circumstances will almost certainly render it inappropriate within months.

Which brings us back to spans of control. We have for some years used and evolved a diagnostic technique for reviewing management structures, whose principles can then be used to design a new structure with appropriate 'spans of control'. The approach is illustrated in Figure 16.

The technique is based on the principle that a manager's job consists of *own work* and *supervision* of subordinates. The supervisory loading in the job

Figure 16 Management 'spans of control'

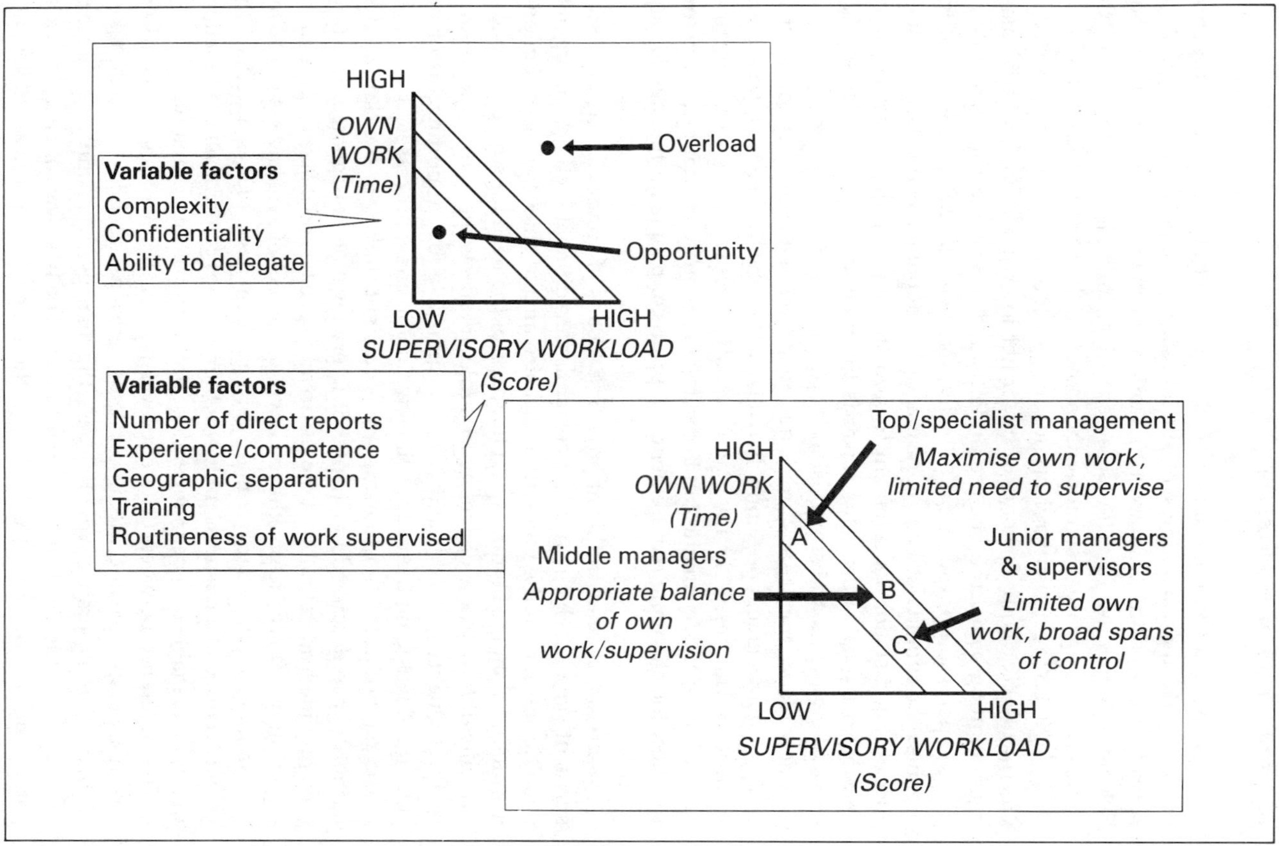

Variable factors

Complexity
Confidentiality
Ability to delegate

Variable factors

Number of direct reports
Experience/competence
Geographic separation
Training
Routineness of work supervised

HIGH

OWN
WORK
(Time)

LOW

SUPERVISORY WORKLOAD
(Score)

HIGH

Overload

Opportunity

Top/specialist management

*Maximise own work,
limited need to supervise*

Junior managers
& supervisors

*Limited own
work, broad spans
of control*

HIGH

OWN WORK
(Time)

A

B

C

Middle managers

*Appropriate balance
of own
work/supervision*

LOW

SUPERVISORY WORKLOAD
(Score)

HIGH

depends not only on the number of subordinates but also on the complexity of the work, the capabilities of the individuals supervised, geographical spread, and so forth. 'Own work' is work that a manager cannot (or will not) delegate. A method of self-assessment plots individual managers on the chart. Those appearing significantly above the line are overloaded – either they have too great a supervisory loading, or too much own work, or both. One or other or both elements of his or her job will suffer. Similarly, managers plotting below the line are underloaded, and could therefore take on more supervision or own work. Finally, managers at different levels of the organisation should normally appear at different points on the diagonal line – specialist and senior management towards the top, and junior management and departmental supervisors towards the bottom, reflecting different balances of own work and supervision.

A new management structure is designed from the bottom up, only establishing a management position when it is justified by the needs of those being managed. The result is invariably a flatter, more responsive structure. Furthermore, the technique can be used continuously to adapt the structure to reflect the changing requirements of groups of people for managerial support.

We no longer refer to this approach as 'spans of control'. Instead we use spans of *support*. This is not just semantics: traditional methods of organisation design start at the top, with the chairman and chief executive. Building a structure from the bottom up on the basis of the need for support implies a radically different view of a manager's role. It reflects the role of the manager in Total Quality as leader and coach, responsible for supporting his or her staff and developing their capabilities within business processes.

The method has a further important element, linked to the 'knowledge/ authority' gap described in Chapter 5. Every level of management must not only provide leadership but it must also add specific and *different* value to the organisation. This concerns the 'own work' element of a manager's job. Why, for example, should a factory manager have a manager? He is, in effect, the chief executive of a business unit, whether or not it contains all the functions that would enable it to be independent of the rest of the company.

The difference between different levels of management should lie in the strategic perspective and the timescale of decisions. Each level should take a clearly different perspective, otherwise the manager will simply duplicate or interfere with the decisions of subordinates. The best way of ensuring delegation and empowerment is to design the possibility of upward delegation out of the structure, by giving more senior managers a clearly different remit. In building the structure from the bottom up, we start with empowerment, taking responsibility for decisions up the structure *only when there is a good reason for doing so.*

Rank Xerox, winners of the first European Quality Award in 1992, have adopted a similar approach to organisation:

> 'Key elements of the approach include . . . organisation design from the micro-enterprise unit out – we are turning the process of organization design upside down. Instead of always designing top-down, we start with the micro-enterprise unit which deals directly with the product, service, and customer and then work out. . . .
>
> Self-management – Empower people to design/redesign their own work processes and practices, including work flows, assignments, hiring and firing, etc. Where possible, take the supervisory roles out. One manager might have a number of teams. He or she can't run them day by day. The manager has to be a coach, consultant, supporter and resource.'[14]

Functional parochialism

Every profession has its institutes. Some, like accountants, have several. They bestow enormous advantages, including the development of professional competence and excellence, standards, ethics and codes of conduct. However, there is a risk that institutes encourage professional parochialism. Professional parochialism is not the cause, but merely one of the factors that reinforce functional parochialism within companies. It is unhelpful when people matters become the exclusive preserve of the Personnel function, when the application of Information Technology is restricted to the IS department, when accounting is understood only by the Finance function, when product design is owned by Product Engineering, or when understanding of customer needs and customer contact are the job of Sales and Marketing alone.

Parochialism has many subtle causes, but the most powerful is simply intolerance of mistakes. The greatest barrier to cooperation and progress is the widely held view that a mistake is a bad thing, and deserves blame. Blame generates an all-pervasive, cultural aversion to risk – and a strong tendency to put everything in writing to cover one's backside.

> *The IT Director of a financial services company insisted that an extra (pink) copy be made of every memo or letter produced within the division. The 'pinks'*

were collated into a file, which was walked round the management team by a messenger every morning.

Mistakes are by definition unintentional. Punishment is a pointless and sterile response. Even making the same mistake twice is unintentional, and rare. Total Quality is concerned with *prevention* of mistakes: this means establishing and maintaining standards and procedures that will avoid them, and controls that will detect them until such time as the process can be made robust. Such controls should not be confused with controls aimed at prevention or detection of fraud or malice: fraud and malice are not mistakes – they are deliberate.

Innovation requires experiment, and experiments sometimes fail. Whether they fail or not, experiments provide knowledge, and knowledge is the lifeblood of progress.

Systems of motivation and reward

In 1968 the *Harvard Business Review* published an article by Frederick Herzberg entitled *'One More Time: How Do You Motivate Employees?'*[15]. Since its publication, the article has generated more requests for reprints than any other *HBR* article.

In it, Herzberg published his motivation-hygiene theory of job attitudes, which was 'first drawn from an examination of events in the lives of engineers and accountants. At least 16 other investigations, using a wide variety of populations [were subsequently] . . . completed, making the original research one of the most replicated studies in the field of job attitudes'. Since then a great deal more practical and academic research has corroborated Herzberg's basic conclusions.

Two key conclusions are relevant here. The first is that:

'the factors involved in producing job satisfaction are separate and distinct from the factors that lead to job dissatisfaction. . . . It follows that the two feelings are not opposites of each other. The opposite of job satisfaction is not job dissatisfaction but, rather, no job satisfaction; and similarly, the opposite of job dissatisfaction is not job satisfaction, but no job dissatisfaction.'

The second is that:

'The growth or *motivator* factors that are intrinsic to the job are:

achievement, recognition for achievement, the work itself, responsibility, and growth or self-advancement. The dissatisfaction–avoidance or *hygiene* factors that are extrinsic to the job include: company policy and administration, supervision, interpersonal relationships, working conditions, salary, status, and security.'

A simple illustration of the concept in practice is that pay has very little capacity to motivate; however, when used as an instrument of company policy, it holds enormous potential to *demotivate*.

A bank decided to restrict the annual pay award to its staff to 2 per cent, on the grounds that the bank's performance and the recession did not justify more. Unfortunately, the Chief Executive also decided that only one of the following percentage increases could be awarded to any individual: 0, 2, 5 or 10 per cent. He saw this simply as the first implementation of a stated policy of relating pay to performance. Staff reaction was extremely negative. However, not only was there no objection to the ceiling of 2 per cent but the emphasis of their feedback was that given the circumstances, staff would have understood if there had been no increase at all. There were several pointed questions about top management salaries.

The 0, 2, 5, 10 per cent implementation not only confused the message but it also had profound effects on staff motivation:

- All departments were expected to have a number of 'poor performers', to whom punishment was administered in the form of a 0 per cent increase.
- Any manager who ventured to suggest that this was not the case, or inappropriate, lacked toughness and was himself therefore by definition a 'poor performer'.
- In order to be able to afford to pay 5 per cent or 10 per cent to some individuals, a manager *needed* a certain number of 'poor performers'. The system thereby gave an incentive to managers to polarise staff performance, and to find enough 'poor performers' to fund a nice increase for the shakers and movers.
- Some individuals therefore gained at the expense of others, with whom they nevertheless needed to cooperate all year round.
- The system implied that individuals 'perform' in isolation from others, not as part of a system or process.
- The bank had just spent six months telling people that there was a new management style in which management would think before they acted,

encourage teamwork and avoid blaming others. Management credibility was destroyed and the fear culture reinstated at a stroke.

The story speaks volumes for attitudes that are buried deep in the culture of many companies. Performance-related pay is one of the single most destructive instruments of policy that exists in British corporate culture. If for no other reason, this is because punishment is implicit in its operation – punishment of individuals who are victims of processes whose failures are outside their control. It is destructive of teamwork and cooperation, degrades both assessor and assessed, and builds the fear of failure into the business culture.

There is a better way. Any system of staff remuneration should recognise that there is a key distinction between *capability* and *performance:*

- *Individuals* should be paid for their *capability* – that is, their actual or potential value to the company. Market rate will influence this. People should be recruited on the basis of their capability, and then trained and given experience in order to improve their capability. People should be promoted to managerial or supervisory positions on the basis of their leadership capability. People with technical capabilities in any field can be paid more, and promoted, but not to management/supervisory positions. Individuals should *never* be rewarded for *personal* performance.
- Only *groups* of people (and preferably the whole company) should be rewarded for *performance;* how much people get paid for performance should depend on how much profit the *whole company* makes. Performance depends fundamentally on teamwork and cooperation: the ability to foster teamwork and cooperation is therefore the most important element of leadership.

All staff in a company should be grouped according to *market rate* for their job (capability). All staff with the same capability, regardless of age, should be paid the same. An annual 'inflation' increase should never be automatic, but depend instead on whether or not the company is sufficiently profitable to pay it. There is no reason for changes to salary to be an annual event.

If the company makes a profit, a share should be paid to *all* staff in the company strictly in proportion to their salary.

It will appear controversial to suggest that salary rates should be adjusted up *or down* to reflect market rate, and to reflect the fact that some capabilities will decline in usefulness to a company, and that this should be reflected in declining levels of pay. Moreover, we do not propose that this should ever be done over the short term. However, the point is that management have an obligation to plan manpower resources in such a way as to allow for retraining and redeployment of staff into new jobs with capabilities that *are* in demand. In the long term this also encourages an organisation to have fewer, more capable people, rather than more, less capable people.

This approach to pay and reward does not discourage cooperation and teamwork, and puts pressure on management to develop their staff's capabilities.

There is a useful analogy here with a football team. Footballers are recruited for their individual talent and potential. They are trained and given experience to develop that talent. If their capability is great – a Lineker or a Gascoigne – they are paid more, and there are highly publicised market rates for top footballers. However, in a match the player who scores a goal never does it alone: he depends on teamwork. Individuality and flair provide the edge – cooperation and teamwork provide the platform, without which personal ability has no room for expression.

We can take this further, by recognising that personal attitudes and behaviour are critical. If the individual genius is a poor team player, then the efforts of the whole team are frustrated. Moreover, personal attitude and behaviour can adversely affect a player's own capability. If he makes intemperate tackles that result in a broken leg, or gets drunk in a night club, he damages his own capability. There is a good argument for paying him less as a result.

In his book *Dr Deming: the Man who Taught the Japanese about Quality*, Rafael Aguayo[16] gives a powerful illustration of effective leadership, again from the world of sport:

'. . . the following advertisement by Panhandle Eastern Corporation, which appeared in the *Wall Street Journal* and other newspapers in 1986, indicates . . . a coaching philosophy [that] has had enormous success over a long period of time in university-level team sports. The text is reproduced below in its entirety.

JOHN WOODEN, ON STAYING POWER

John Wooden is the only man ever enshrined in the basketball Hall of Fame as both player and coach. He retired after 40 years of coaching, leaving a record unparalleled in American sport.

During his 27 years as coach of UCLA, his teams never had a losing season. In his last 12 years there, they won ten national championships, seven of those in succession, and still hold the world's record for the longest winning streak in any major sport – 88 games bridging four seasons.

Although retired now, he still conducts coaching clinics and basketball camps, and lectures widely.

Peaks create valleys
"I believe for every artificial peak you create, you also create valleys. When you get too high for anything, emotion takes over and consistency of performance is lost and you will be unduly affected when adversity comes. I emphasized constant improvement and steady performance.

"I have often said, 'The mark of a true champion is to always perform near your own level of competency.' We were able to do that by never being satisfied with the past and always planning for what was to come. I believe that failure to prepare is preparing to fail. This constant focus on the future is one reason we continued staying near the top once we got there.

Develop yourself, don't worry about opponents
"I probably scouted opponents less than any coach in the country. Less than most high school coaches. I don't need to know that this forward likes to drive the outside. You're not supposed to give the outside to any forward whenever he tries it. Sound offensive and defensive principles apply to any style of play.

"Rather than having my teams prepare to play a certain team each week, I prepared to play anybody. I didn't want my players worrying about the other fellows. I wanted them executing the sound offensive and defensive principles we taught in practice.

There's no pillow as soft as a clear conscience
To me, success isn't outscoring someone, it's the peace of mind that comes from self-satisfaction in knowing you did your best. That's something each individual must determine for himself. You can fool others, but you can't fool yourself.

"Many people are surprised to learn that in 27 years at UCLA, I never once talked about winning. Instead I would tell my players before games, 'When it's over, I want your head up. And there's only one way your head can be up, that's for you to know, not me, that you gave the best effort of which you're capable. If you do that, then the score doesn't really matter, although I have a feeling that if you do that, the score will be to your liking.' I honestly believe that in not stressing winning as such, we won more than we would have if I'd stressed outscoring opponents.

Why do so many people dread adversity, when it is only through adversity that we grow stronger
"There's no great fun, satisfaction or joy derived from doing something that's easy. Failure is never fatal, but failure to change might be. Your strength as an individual depends on, and will be in direct proportion to how you react to both praise and criticism. If you become too concerned about either, the effect on you is sure to be adverse.

The main ingredient of stardom
"I always taught players that the main ingredient of stardom is the rest of the team. It's amazing how much can be accomplished if no one cares who gets the credit. That's why I was as concerned with a player's character as I was with his ability.

"While it may be possible to reach the top of one's profession on sheer ability, it is impossible to stay there without hard work and character. One's character may be quite different from one's reputation.

"Your character is what you really are. Your reputation is only what others think you are. I made a determined effort to evaluate character. I looked for young men who would play the game hard, but clean, and who would always be trying to improve themselves to help the team. Then, if their ability warranted it, the championships would take care of themselves."

One sentence from Mr Wooden's essay particularly helps to illuminate some of the ill effects of merit systems and incentive pay plans that foster competition among people who should be working together: "*It's amazing how much can be accomplished if no one cares who gets the credit.*"'

Objecting to performance related pay for individuals does *not* mean ignoring individual personality, talent and ability. On the contrary, leadership means developing individual capability, and enabling individuals to contribute to the team effort to their highest potential.

Regrettably, many systems of reward and promotion do the opposite: they encourage competition and discourage cooperation. Internal competition may be a spur (the euphemism is 'friendly rivalry') but it is an inappropriate one when the most important characteristic that is needed in a leader is the ability to foster teamwork and develop the capabilities of others.

The problem of motivation and reward does not stop with systems of pay and promotion. There are many aspects of corporate life that drive behaviour, and therefore become mechanisms of incentive and reward. The following in particular play a major part in influencing how people behave, yet they are seldom seen as instruments of motivation:

- conventional budgeting and management accounts;
- internal cross-charging;
- appraisal systems;
- training policy.

Conventional budgeting and management accounts

Budgeting should be the method by which an organisation *allocates resources* to business processes, to establish the necessary capability to produce forecast outputs, and to invest in the future.

If budgeting is allocation of resources, it is not – by definition – a method of cost control. However, in many organisations, it becomes a surrogate for cost control, in the absence of better methods of cost management. Control of costs is the *result* of managing cross-functional business processes effectively.

In the majority of British companies, the monthly management accounts are the only regular information about the business that managers receive. Conventional management accounts usually record departmental input costs, compare them with the budget, and show the difference as a variance. In many organisations, 'meeting budget' is an overriding personal objective for managers.

Focus on variances leads to the belief that once a variance is eliminated, an objective has been achieved. This confuses inputs with outputs, so that managers are held accountable for 'meeting budget'. The purpose of the budget is to decide what resources to *supply,* and once this decision is made, the need is to understand how such resources are used and the resulting capacity issues. The budget does not constitute the 'correct cost', and meeting budget does not imply that management have done the right thing.

Misuse of budgets in this way generates all kinds of behaviour that conflict with the interests of the organisation and its customers.

- A sudden increase in sales revenue budgets reveals them as targets, not forecasts for the purposes of allocating resource and building capability. If it were that easy, why were they not at that level before?

- If budgeted revenue is treated as a target, rather than a forecast, people will relax once it is achieved. If it is impossible to achieve, they may give up.
- It is not uncommon for salesmen with monthly quotas to hold orders over until the following month.
- Higher than usual levels of both capital and revenue expenditure in the last two months of a financial year often indicate that departments are trying to avoid underspending the budget, for fear of a reduction in the following year.
- Disputes about 'who will pay' for an investment or resource that is patently cost-justified result from an overriding incentive to come in under departmental budget.
- Divisions and departments often overstate estimated costs in the conviction that Head Office will cut the budget anyway.
- Intolerance of any attempt by an operating unit to budget for a loss often demonstrates preoccupation with short-term results.

An extreme example of the misuse of budgets is highlighted by the following report from *The Independent* of 24 August 1992:

'Food will reach Somalia too late

The massive consignment of food the United States has promised for the millions of Somalis facing starvation because of famine and civil war will not arrive in time. Thousands of lives are on the brink of death.

On 14th August President Bush ordered 145,000 tons of food aid to be made available, and the White House said the Pentagon would begin airlifts "as soon as possible".

However, the shipments will be covered by the budget for the next fiscal year, beginning on 1 October, according to the US Embassy spokesman in the Kenyan capital, and so are unlikely to be at sea before mid-October. They could not be expected to reach Somalia before early November.'

Budgets can kill.

Deming[17] has asserted that the most important numbers for any business are the values that attach to happy customers, quality improvements, teamwork, pride in workmanship and so forth. He refers to these as 'unknown and unknowable'. They must be taken into account by management. The greatest danger comes from relying on 'visible figures' alone to run the business – by which he means conventional financial and management accounts.

Management accounts are necessary, to track costs and to make them available for analysis along with other data, to provide management with information about the performance of business processes.

In recent years, something of a revolution has started in the field of management accounting. Activity Based Costing (ABC) acquired prominence in the late 1980s, particularly following publication in 1987 of Professors Kaplan and Johnson's book *Relevance Lost: the Rise and Fall of Management Accounting*.[18] Activity Based Costing not only addresses the need for improved methods of product and customer costing but also recognises the importance of cross-functional processes and the information management require to manage them effectively.[19]

Internal cross charging

Most companies attempt to deal with the problem of process management through internal cross charging. Recognising that one department's costs are influenced or driven by the demands made on it by others, the accounting solution is to make them pay for the service, on the grounds that this will make the internal customer cost conscious – with the added benefit that it will impose 'market disciplines' on the supplier of the service. There are few more effective methods of introducing misunderstandings, distrust, dissension and defensive behaviour into an organisation. These are sticks, not carrots, and the effect is never to generate a constructive, cooperative dialogue between managers.

There are several barrier-building consequences of internal cross charging:

- The administrative overhead activity involved adds no value.
- A cross charge is seldom made at cost – it is usually a *price*: this makes the information useless for purposes such as product costing. The most extreme example is cross charging of mainframe computer costs. The charging algorithm is incomprehensible to anyone outside computer services, and arbitrary (for technical reasons which are both boring and outside the scope of this discussion). The department receiving the charge treats it as a cost, and has to assume it to be accurate – which it is not, even though it may appear with two decimal places.
- Cross charging usually fragments a cost, which thereby reduces understanding of what drives it.
- Cross charging often implies that a cost is variable. Hitting the 'Enter' key on

a computer terminal less often may result in a lower cross charge, but the cost of the hardware and software has already been incurred. Besides, why implement a charge that discourages usage of a system, when presumably it should be *encouraged* on the basis that it is a better way of working than the old manual system?

- Cross charges are sometimes imposed to 'discourage wasteful use of resources': this is a poor substitute for effective communication and process management.
- Cross charges encourage focus on function, not process.

Cross charging should not be confused with analysis of costs for allocation purposes when calculating product and customer costs. Cross charging is the transfer of costs between cost centres. Cost allocation (where cause and effect are understood) and apportionment (where it is not) are important concepts in product costing and do not depend on cross charging.

Appraisal systems

There are two types of appraisal system: individual performance appraisal, and capability assessment.

There is little that can be said in favour of formal individual performance appraisal. Personal attitudes and behaviour, which are vitally important to people who must work closely with others in a team, should never be the subject of a formal annual interview. A manager and the individual's colleagues must address these issues as they arise, in the normal course of day-to-day work.

Individual performance appraisal has a destructive effect even beyond the problem of performance-related pay, since punishment is built into the system.

> *A manufacturing company's performance appraisal system required every one of its 2,300 employees to be appraised annually in May, before the annual pay award in July. The Personnel Director's statistical ability led him to recognise that the world is a normal distribution, and that in any sample of people, there would be different capabilities – and therefore different levels of 'performance'. Each employee was rated on a scale of 1 to 10 (very poor to outstanding), and every function was required to demonstrate a spread of performance ratings across the whole scale. This was to prevent managers 'being over protective of their staff' by rating them too highly, this being statistically improbable. Any employee scoring 5 or less received no 'merit' increase in salary, the maximum for which was 2 per cent. More significantly, any employee rated 3 or less in two consecutive appraisals was given a formal warning of dismissal unless his*

or her 'performance' improved. Morale was disastrously low: staff turnover in a recession-hit region of the country was four times the sector average, and graduate retention within the first two years of joining the company was less than 50 per cent.

People will do whatever is necessary to earn reward or to avoid punishment, which encourages behaviour which is at the expense of others. Self-defence generates blame, and blame is destructive of morale.

Capability assessment on the other hand has value, when it is focused on the action that management will initiate to improve a person's capability. It encourages management to plan, and provides a structured way of defining what is needed from the training function.

Training policy

Training is a core activity. Properly directed and focused, training creates future capability. Nothing is more important to the long-term success of a business.

Many companies see training as a necessary evil, or something that the government should do. Training often stops at middle-manager level, perhaps in the belief that climbing the management ladder is evidence of increasing wisdom, knowledge and original thought.

The newly appointed Management Development Manager in a large manufacturing company discovered that among the top three levels of management, including the Board, not one person had attended an external conference or training course in the previous three years.

The Director of Management Services in a large financial services company banned attendance at all technical training courses and conferences lasting longer than two days, on the grounds that 'all training courses are excuses for social jollies at the company's expense'. Management training courses were banned altogether, on the grounds that they were 'all run by smart-alecs teaching grandmother to suck eggs'.

In a life assurance company, actuaries were found to pursue their own professional training with vigour, to the extent that the actuarial function appeared to cease functioning during professional examinations. However, actuaries almost never attended internal management courses. It transpired that within the actuarial function, management training was regarded as remedial: being sent on one amounted to serious personal criticism. In contrast, training courses for salesmen were regarded as a reward: only salesmen who had achieved their targets consistently for a year were allowed to attend a two-week head office course on advanced salesmanship!

Training concerns development of specific skills and knowledge to carry out specific tasks; maintaining standards through acquisition of knowledge about procedures and processes; development of leadership, interpersonal and other behavioural skills; challenging complacency and accepted wisdom; and above all, generating a culture of continuous learning that goes hand in hand with continuous improvement.

Summary

In many organisations, Total Quality is seen as enormously attractive but difficult to implement. This is simply because the barriers lie in those elements of corporate life that people take for granted: management hierarchy and status, pay and reward, appraisal systems, change mechanisms and methods of accounting and 'control'.

Questioning these causes a great deal of uncertainty. Many people in senior positions got there because they played by rules that are now described as irrelevant or positively counter productive. Above all, Total Quality challenges *management*.

Managers are no longer required to *control* other people, nor to be accountable for their 'own patch'. They are being asked to trust, to encourage, to lead, to coach, to cooperate, and to accept mistakes. Penalty and blame have been withdrawn from their armoury of management weapons. Above all, managers are being asked to accept *obligations* towards others – in particular towards their staff and colleagues in other parts of the business – and therefore to replace such weapons with behavioural skills that are quite different from the ones they used to become managers in the first place.

CHAPTER 7

Implementation

> '"Cheshire Puss," Alice began, rather timidly . . . "would you tell me please, which way ought I to go from here?"
> "That depends a good deal on where you want to get to," said the Cat.
> "I don't much care where—" said Alice.
> "Then it doesn't matter which way you go," said the Cat.
> "—so long as I get somewhere," Alice added as an explanation.
> "Oh, you're sure to do that," said the Cat, "if only you walk long enough."'
>
> *Lewis Carroll*

Like Alice, companies deciding to implement Total Quality are faced with a choice of alternatives. A proper start to Total Quality is essential. Early problems or a loss of momentum will have adverse consequences. Apathy and cynicism will quickly overcome initial enthusiasm. Total Quality must win significant benefits quickly, not merely to justify the decision to initiate it, but to provide momentum by demonstrating to everyone that the time and effort they invest produces significant results.

Confusingly, there are two camps on implementation – one camp favours a culture change, the other a project by project approach. Both claim the support of one or other of the eminent quality gurus – Deming, Juran, Crosby, *et al.*

We argue that a combination of both is needed. If organisations attempt to undertake projects without at the same time changing the culture, many of those projects will ultimately fail. The reason is simple: the problems that caused the project to be identified in the first place almost certainly require cross-functional cooperation, enthusiasm to participate and the objective involvement of management in order to solve them. Without these ingredients, projects will be viewed with suspicion by those whom they affect, particularly managers, and the barriers will go up. The initiative will peter out.

If, on the other hand, organisations attempt to change the culture without at the same time undertaking projects, they fall into another trap: telling people the attitudes and behaviour they should adopt towards customers, their peers and those who report to them will not in itself result in a long-term culture change. People need a great deal of support to convert the theory of how they should behave into the practice of precisely what they should do differently the morning after the course or workshop on which they were taught how to behave ended. Apart from the problems of *how* to behave differently, people need reassurance that their new behaviour will not be seen as a sign of weakness – or madness – by their colleagues and, in particular, by more senior managers.

We therefore believe that the way round the problem is a combination of culture change *and* projects. People need to have the new culture explained to them and immediately have the opportunity to put the theory into practice. Trainers refer to this as the 'teachable time' – the time at which the teaching has an impact because those being taught have an immediate use for what they are learning.

Moreover, because projects, to be successful, need the positive involvement of all the people across the organisation that they impact, the *simultaneous* participation of large numbers of people throughout the organisation is required. Otherwise projects will founder because some of the participants will not understand their new role and will consequently block progress.

This simultaneous involvement of large numbers of people clearly requires a large commitment of resources. The initiative therefore needs careful timing, and certainly cannot be done until the senior management group has made its own commitment to Total Quality, and has agreed to proceed. We describe one approach to an improvement project in Stage 2 of implementation later in this chapter.

The right organisational culture is the essential ingredient of Total Quality. Continuous improvement happens because employees become committed to producing good quality in the work they do, and continuously seek ways to do even better. That commitment can only be obtained if people care about what customers want and believe that their organisation cares about them.

In return, people can care deeply about the organisations they work for. They can achieve things way beyond expectations – or contribute just the minimum that is required. If people fail to be creative or enthusiastic or to take the initiative it does not mean that they are not capable of doing so. It means that they choose not to: the 'culture' of the organisation is inhibiting them. Organisations that treat their people as little more than another expendable resource inspire no belief or fulfilment in those unfortunate enough to work for them. Even the term some organisations use for their people betrays a subconscious attitude. We dislike the use of the term 'human resource' because it seems to place people in the same category as any other resource to be used or discarded on a corporate whim.

The scale of change required for an organisation depends to what extent the present culture of the organisation is in conflict with the values and beliefs inherent in Total Quality. For some organisations, the transition is merely difficult. For most, it is extremely difficult.

The transition to Total Quality

The problem with trying to establish models for the introduction of Total Quality is that there is remarkable diversity in the approaches taken by successful organisations. There is also often a strong element of organic development and sometimes luck.

Total Quality frequently has very modest roots – perhaps just a few managers trying to work together using quality improvement tools to work on a common problem. If these attempts are successful, other managers want to be involved, and there is a gradual mushrooming of teams and the use of improvement techniques.

In other companies a charismatic leader has been able to achieve a transformation in performance through an inspiring vision, strong personal commitment and a determination to introduce change. Some of the most successful implementations of Total Quality have originated in this way.

In truth, there is no 'cook book' for success. Organisations are too different from one another for a single recipe to work best in all circumstances. What is right in one company may fail in another. The secret is to find an approach that is a comfortable fit.

In looking at the experience of many different companies that have introduced Total Quality, we can identify six separate stages of development, each of which has its own set of characteristics, and at each of which different elements of Total Quality become relevant.

This chapter describes a series of implementation steps typically carried out at each of the six stages. This is not a rigid specification. Some steps may be carried out at a different stage from that suggested here, or perhaps not at all. Others will need to be added to accommodate the unique nature of each organisation.

Figure 17 The transition to Total Quality

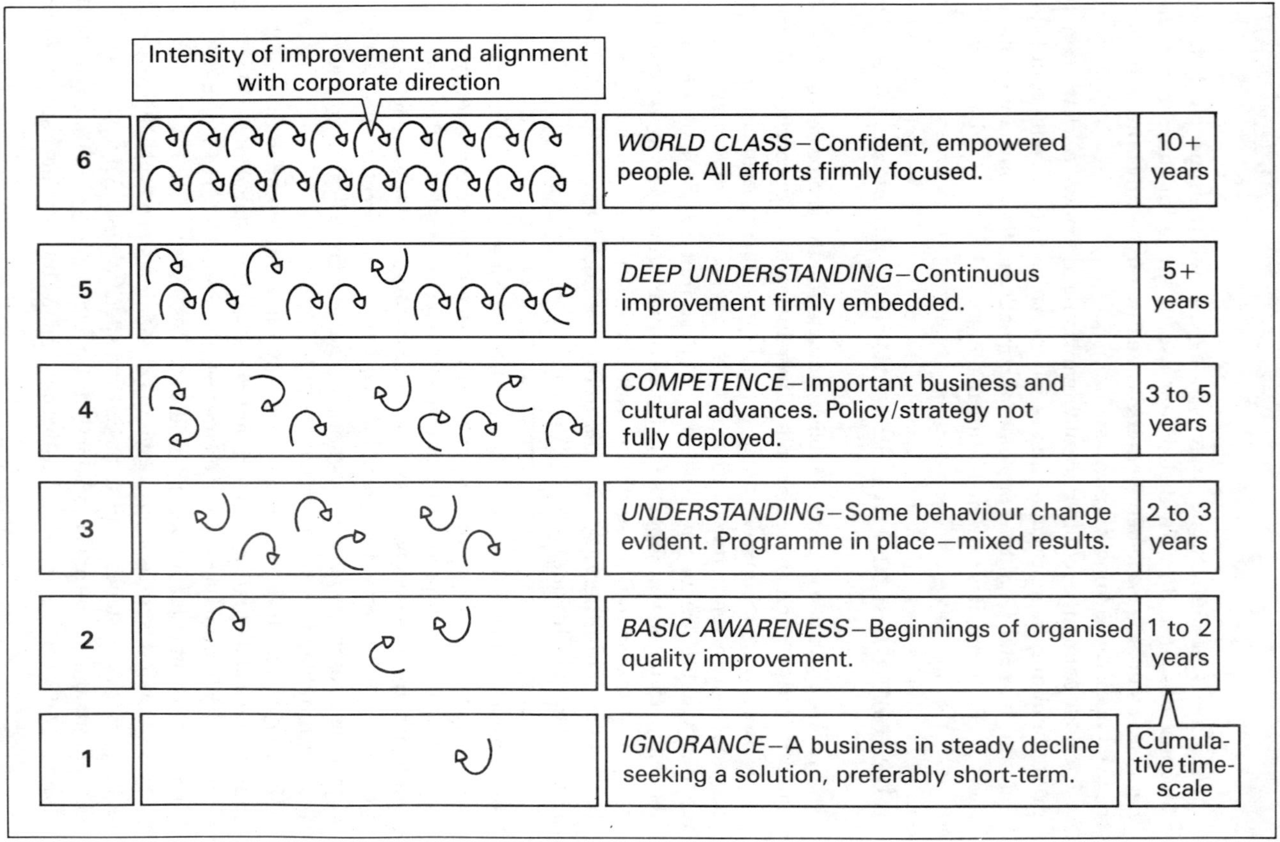

Intensity of improvement and alignment with corporate direction

Level	Description	Cumulative time-scale
6	*WORLD CLASS* – Confident, empowered people. All efforts firmly focused.	10+ years
5	*DEEP UNDERSTANDING* – Continuous improvement firmly embedded.	5+ years
4	*COMPETENCE* – Important business and cultural advances. Policy/strategy not fully deployed.	3 to 5 years
3	*UNDERSTANDING* – Some behaviour change evident. Programme in place – mixed results.	2 to 3 years
2	*BASIC AWARENESS* – Beginnings of organised quality improvement.	1 to 2 years
1	*IGNORANCE* – A business in steady decline seeking a solution, preferably short-term.	

Stage 1 – Ignorance

Most UK companies still have a results-oriented, short-term outlook. The relationship between managers and staff is usually characterised by distrust on both sides, with little cooperation. Quality improvement activity is often limited to quality assurance, and is highly product-focused. The concept of quality as applied to finance, sales and other 'overhead' areas is probably unheard of. Companies at this stage are usually slowly losing the battle against more agile competitors, and suffering a gradual erosion of market share. Their managers will be casting around for a solution, but usually they will be looking for very short-term results – particularly cost-cutting. The prospects without a transformation in performance are not promising.

The transition to the next stage usually only occurs when someone decides to champion Total Quality. The role is not an easy one, because it requires persistence and resilience, especially in the early days. In larger organisations, or organisations with several locations, a network of champions may be needed.

The champion is not necessarily a charismatic, a visionary or even an intellectual character. More often, he or she is a pragmatic pioneer who seizes on Total Quality as the 'idea whose time has come' and enthusiastically pushes it to fruition. Resilience is a necessary quality, because pioneers tend to get shot at.

A Director of a large manufacturing company became interested in Total Quality. Over a period of several months, he read dozens of books and numerous articles to consolidate his understanding. He then felt sufficiently confident to badger his CEO to read just one book. The CEO initially resisted – he was too busy. But the champion persisted. He highlighted relevant parts of the book for the CEO to read to make it less time-consuming. The CEO finally agreed to read the highlights. Then he read the whole book. Then he read it again and made his own summary for his top management team to read. The director then sent him the best of the articles he had read. This prompted the CEO to visit an award-winning quality company. The first rays of sunshine were breaking through. The organisation now had two champions.

Other pressures can also trigger a commitment to Total Quality. Many large organisations are now insisting that their suppliers be accredited to BS 5750 *and* be committed to Total Quality. (We compare BS 5750 and Total Quality in Appendix B.) Another trigger can be the success achieved by a competitor through Total Quality. In this stage, an organisation begins to understand the implications of Total Quality, and begins to commit resources to its introduction.

The primary need is to secure sufficient management commitment for some resources and some commitment to education and training in order to move the organisation to the next stage.

There are a number of things a company can do to begin to acquire an awareness of Total Quality:

- reading;
- conferences;
- workshops and courses;
- visits to successful Total Quality companies;
- pilot quality improvement projects.

Stage 2 – Basic awareness

This is the key stage of transition. Get it right, and Total Quality has a chance. Get it wrong, and it may take years to recover the necessary credibility to start again.

At this stage, a company will develop a form of Total Quality, but is likely to see it as a programme or a project rather than a continuous process that is firmly embedded in the culture of the organisation. Improvements are typically directed at a limited number of very specific problem areas, resulting in participation by only a minority of people. There will be little or no change in management behaviour and perhaps little perceived involvement of senior management.

The successful transition to the next stage often depends on the success of these first few improvement projects. Without some encouraging results in a reasonably short timescale, there exists a real risk that management will lose interest, and look for an alternative solution to their problems.

In this stage, an organisation commits serious resources to quality improvement and begins to reap the rewards. By the end of the stage, the organisation should have defined a plan and structure for Total Quality, but will have a limited view of how Total Quality will develop over the long term. This stage typically sees:

- an assessment of readiness;
- an assessment of the opportunity to increase revenue;
- an assessment of the opportunity to reduce the cost of quality;
- an improvement project to initiate transition;

- a coordinated quality awareness, education and training programme;
- the establishment of a 'Quality organisation'.

Assessment of readiness

This is an assessment of the prevailing organisation culture. It is designed to identify barriers to Total Quality, so that the most appropriate approach to education and training can be devised.

It is also used to develop a plan for the implementation of Total Quality, identifying the best approach, priorities and timing.

A series of questionnaires carefully designed to identify gaps, deficiencies and opportunities for quality improvement can form a valuable approach to assessing readiness. Each questionnaire should address one of the foundations: customer focus, continuous improvement, process management, leadership, empowerment, and analytical approach. Analysis of the responses highlights areas that indicate an organisation in tune with Total Quality and aspects of the organisation's culture that are likely to impose a barrier.

Once the factors that are likely to help or hinder the growth of Total Quality in the organisation are known, an approach that builds on the strengths and addresses the weaknesses can be devised.

Assessment of opportunity to increase revenue

This seeks to quantify the benefits of improving quality, to focus improvement efforts and to justify the commitment of resources.

Companies that fail to produce consistently high quality products or service do not retain their share of the market. If a company is consistently able to satisfy its customers and occasionally to delight them, it will be capable of winning business from less effective competitors.

Customer surveys are designed to identify by product/service segment what external customers believe to be important, and how they perceive the organisation in relation to its competitors. The results highlight priorities to improve quality where customer requirements are not being met, as well as the areas where competitive advantage can be won by offering a distinctive service.

We describe the importance of customer surveys in Chapter 4.

The concept of customer surveys can be extended internally. Every function should be asked to prepare a list of all their internal customers, and then to:

- identify what services are provided and to which internal customers;
- establish what their internal requirements for service are;

- understand their perceptions of service quality in relation to their stated needs;
- identify the key areas where the function adds real value to the organisation's processes.

Internal customer surveys are usually carried out in parallel with cost of quality data collection.

Assessment of opportunity to reduce the cost of quality

On average 15–25 per cent or more of people's efforts are wasted. In service companies, the proportion is more typically 30–40 per cent. To this waste, manufacturing companies can add scrap and rectification costs, energy losses, and other manufacturing costs associated directly or indirectly with the failure to carry out activities right first time. The technique to quantify such costs is Cost of Quality data collection.

In a perfect organisation, every activity would be done right first time, every product would be defect-free, and every customer would be delighted. In the real world, mistakes are made, and customers complain. As a result, people undertake activities to put things right. The cost of such activities is referred to as the Cost of Quality. Cost of Quality (COQ) should be more accurately termed the cost of non-quality because it quantifies the effects of wasted effort, materials and energy, and of rework and lost opportunities.

Few organisations are aware of the true penalty of failing to provide consistent quality products and services. In manufacturing companies scrap and rectification costs are only the tip of the iceberg. Inside every organisation there is a hidden office or factory that provides no value-added products or services. It is truly shocking to discover that the equivalent of a third or more of an organisation's people walk in through the front door and then completely waste their working day!

> In the investment arm of a major life assurance company, an analysis of how fund managers spent their time found that fund strategy occupied only 9 per cent of their hours. A much greater proportion was spent in routine administration that added little value in proportion to the effort, and made no use of their special skills. How much better could fund performance have been if only more time had been spent working on the core activities that directly leveraged corporate performance?

Cost of Quality is a tool for understanding work activities, identifying process improvement opportunities, estimating the financial benefits of quality improvement, and monitoring improvement. It recognises three types of quality cost, prevention, appraisal and failure:

1 *Prevention* costs include training, forecasting, problem analysis, data collection, and so forth. These are activities that take place to try to prevent problems and poor quality. Prevention activities stop fire fighting.
2 *Appraisal* costs are incurred when evaluating an output to ensure that it is error-free. This includes inspection costs, checking someone else's work, and so on.
3 *Failure* costs are often divided into internal and external components. Internal failure costs occur when errors or problems are detected before a product is delivered to an external customer. This would include, for example, scrap and rectification, rework, chasing other people for information, and so forth. External failure costs include warranty costs, customer complaints, and recall costs. External failure costs are doubly serious because they are very likely to affect negatively a customer's future purchasing intentions.

Figure 18 (overleaf) illustrates the long-term potential of applying quality improvement techniques. As quality costs are reduced through the elimination of waste, resources are freed up to perform new value-adding activities or to enhance the quality of existing activities. The key to rechannelling time into different activity is a substantial increase in prevention.

The exercise of collecting information on the cost of quality invariably reveals a substantial prize. Just collecting the data provokes questions and generates ideas to reduce the cost of failure. It is a powerful mechanism to gain management's attention, and a way of identifying the areas of waste that will provide the maximum return to the organisation.

A British manufacturing company was facing strong competition from Japanese and German competitors. In their market place, the development cycle time for new products was critical because the first company into the market was able to capture an immediate advantage. The problem was that it took the UK company four years on average to bring a new product to market, compared with two years by their German and 18 months by their Japanese competitors. The company had responded by investing heavily in computer aided design (CAD) to improve the productivity of its development engineers and was recruiting additional ones, but had failed to make significant inroads into cycle time.

An analysis of how development engineers spent their time found a surprisingly low proportion of design and development activity – only 12 per

Figure 18 *Reducing the cost of Quality*

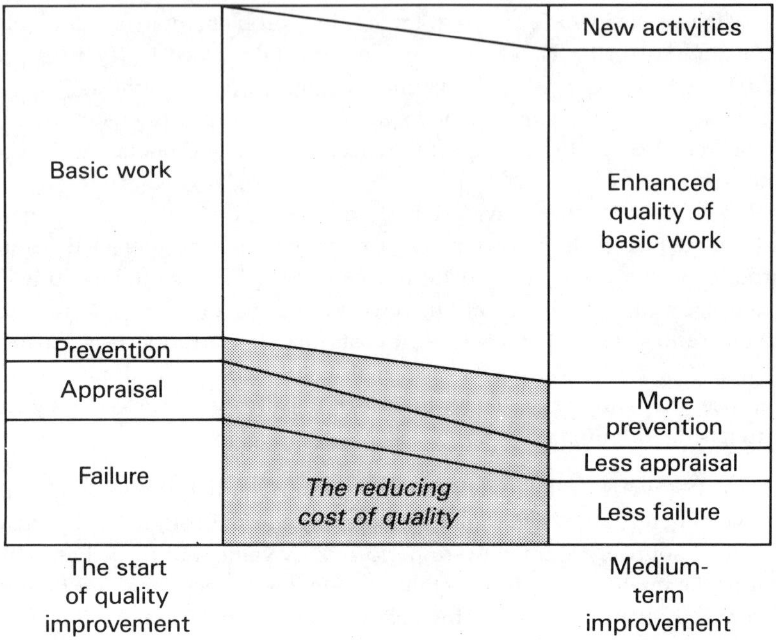

cent of their total effort. Because CAD only improved the productivity of these activities, the overall impact of CAD was very limited. Equally, increasing head count had only a limited effect because new recruits divided their time along the same lines as the rest of the department, contributing only around 12 per cent of their time to the core activity of design and development.

The solution lay in the other activities the engineers were involved in: problems in manufacturing, chasing purchasing for materials, design changes and the like. If these problems could be prevented, precious time would be freed to devote to design and development. Other activities were related to the development process itself – including an extended iterative cycle of prototype manufacture and testing. Investing in technology to support these activities not only released design engineers' time for core activity but it also reduced the development cycle time.

By highlighting the main causes of wasted effort, the Cost of Quality data made it possible to focus on each problem in turn. Over a period of 18 months,

> *the proportion of time spent on design and development increased dramati-
> cally from 12 per cent to 41 per cent; development lead times were halved.*

Organisations seldom collect activity data in what are, regrettably, referred to as the 'overhead areas' – where much value is added. (The Americans describe overheads as 'the burden' – which adds insult). Understanding activities provides immediate insight into the cause and effect of problems.

An improvement project to initiate transition

There is no way of short cutting the various steps and stages of Total Quality: company-wide education and training cannot be omitted, teams have to be trained, a clear plan of how Total Quality is to develop has to be laid down.

However, there comes a critical point in the introduction of Total Quality when the organisation has to take the plunge. Training people in tools and techniques and in the ways they ought to behave is all well and good. But if they perceive no opportunity for putting their training into practice in their real working lives, either because they are too busy or because those with whom they deal – their manager and other departments – wouldn't understand, it will all be a waste of time.

People have to be given an opportunity to put the principles into practice and they need guidance and a structure in which to do so. Furthermore, a large number of them have to be involved, otherwise the attempts to make improvements to any individual group will be frustrated by the indifference of other uninvolved groups with whom they interact.

One way of establishing momentum is through a process that engages staff at all levels in the organisation in generating proposals for change. It involves the whole organisation in a series of steps leading to an action plan to win significant short-term benefits. Figure 19 (overleaf) outlines the approach.

1 *Audit:* the first stage, audit, involves company-wide collection of data to quantify waste and unnecessary activity, and to understand staff percep-tions.

  Audit identifies the main causes of process delays and disruptions; gaps and deficiencies in internal customer service; opportunities to improve efficiency and effectiveness and perceived barriers to Total Quality. Audit also has a strong education and training content, usually limited to top management at this point.

  Audit starts the necessary culture change. People start to understand which activities add value, and which are wasteful. They identify the most

103

Figure 19 *Improvement project to initiate transition*

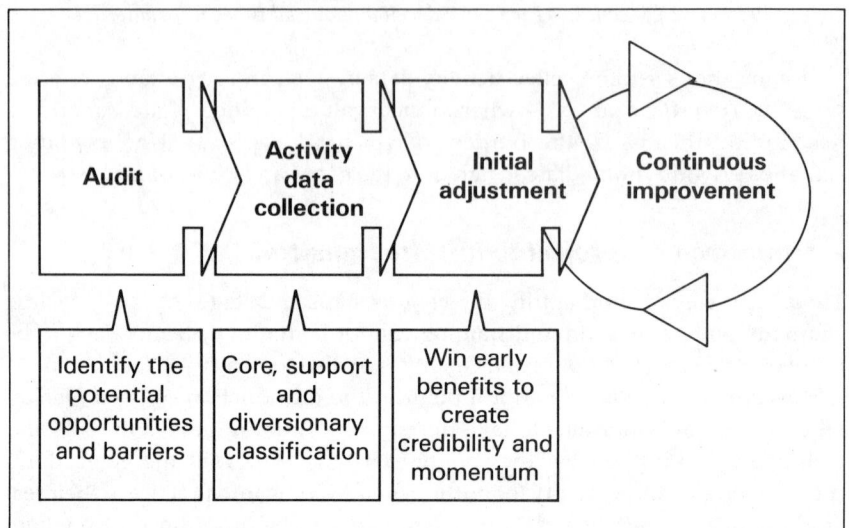

pressing problems facing their function, and identify how improvements in the service they receive from their internal suppliers could reduce unnecessary activity in their own function.

2 *Activity data collection:* a critical step is activity data collection. The whole organisation is broken down into small work groups, each of whom collects a high-level set of data describing their activities. This data describes how effectively and efficiently each work group is able to utilise its resources. Each activity is classified as either *core*, *support* or *diversionary*.

  (a) *Core* activities are those for which the work group exists. These add value to the organisation by providing an essential service to internal or external customers.

  (b) *Support* activities make it possible for a core activity to take place, but do not directly add value. For example, a sales representative's time negotiating with a customer is a core activity. His or her travel time to get to the customer is a necessary, but not value adding, support activity.

  (c) *Diversionary* activity is the result of process failure. It exists because something, somewhere, has gone wrong. Diversionary activities begin with a 'diversionary' verb: chasing, checking, reworking, clarifying, and so forth.

Figure 20 *Activity classification*

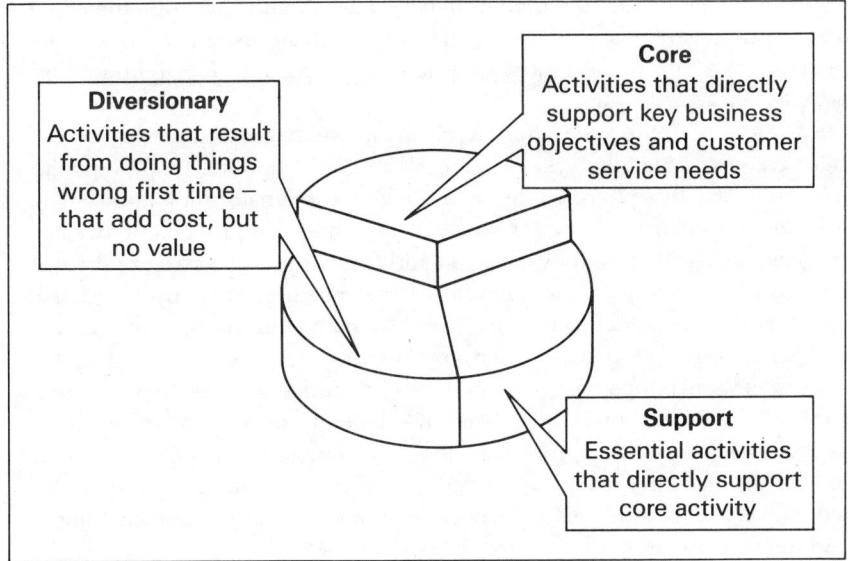

The value of the data is that it forms the agenda for each work group to develop proposals to improve its efficiency and effectiveness. Core and support activities cannot be eliminated, but can they be carried out more efficiently by, for example, improving systems, simplification or streamlining communication channels? Can service levels on services provided to internal customers be *reduced*, thereby freeing up time. Alternatively are there core activities where service levels should be *increased*, thereby eliminating a greater amount of diversionary activity elsewhere? Diversionary activity can seldom be completely eliminated, but how much could be reduced if only internal suppliers could provide a consistently reliable service to their internal customers?

Diversionary activity can only be eliminated by finding the root cause of the problem. Work groups come together using everyone's knowledge of the problem to identify where failures are taking place. By identifying the source of the failure and the associated costs of diversionary activity, a simple cost/benefit analysis can be carried out – the cost of additional effort to get things right first time, compared with the costs of diversionary activity saved elsewhere.

The benefits of working to reduce diversionary activity go far beyond simply eliminating wasted activity. We all know that our core activities are *important.* But it is an unfortunate fact that diversionary activity is by nature often *urgent.* People are diverted from what they should be doing – their core and support activities, into fire fighting and problem fixing. Organisations usually have to put their most experienced people into fire fighting – an activity that adds no value.

3 *Initial adjustment:* the aim of this step is to ensure that each function has the right resources: people, systems, procedures, and training to do a quality job. There are two phases in initial adjustment: brainstorming and review meetings. In brainstorming, groups collect as many improvement ideas as possible, using the data they collected and the analysis of core, support and diversionary activity as the agenda for the meeting. Properly led, these sessions typically generate dozens, or occasionally, hundreds, of ideas. This is the first, crucial step towards empowerment.

In review meetings, the managers of each function meet their internal suppliers and customers to discuss the benefits of alternative levels of service. A feature of this process is the use of dependent benefits: 'we could reduce/eliminate this diversionary activity *if only* . . .'. The aim of the review meeting is to encourage dialogue between internal suppliers and customers and the agreement of new service levels.

A key feature of the process is that it forces consideration of both enhancing *and reducing* service levels on core activities. The result is typically a major rebalancing of resources across the whole of the organisation. Some functions require fewer resources after the process as the result of improvements to systems or the elimination of diversionary activity; others increase their resources in order to improve the quality of their service, thereby eliminating other functions' diversionary activity. Figure 21 illustrates a typical outcome.

The results of these exercises – customer surveys, cost of quality, and the initiation project provide the input to a top management workshop on Total Quality, whose purpose is to define priorities for further improvement in service or elimination of barriers to improvement, and to develop implementation plans.

Quality awareness training

The next step is the development of a comprehensive, properly coordinated quality awareness programme. Education and training is the most important element of any Total Quality initiative. The workshops should provide much more than information: their critical role is to challenge the status quo, to stimulate discussion, and to generate excitement. Unfortunately, many UK

Figure 21 *Typical rebalancing of resources*

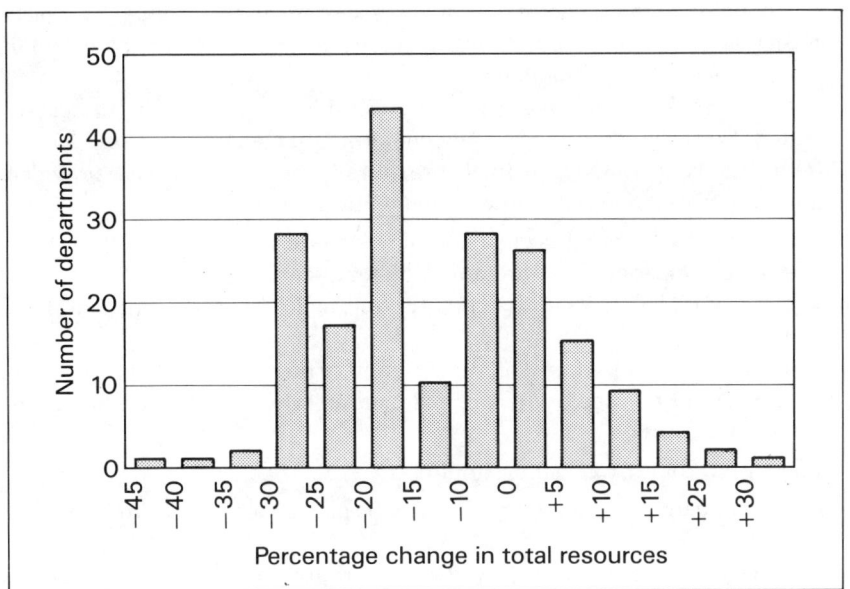

firms pay lip service to the value of training – it is usually one of the first casualties whenever there is a need to restrain spending.

> *Motorola, a true world class competitor, requires that 2.7 per cent of payroll be spent on training. Milliken, another world-class quality company, insist that their top managers spend at least 40 hours per year in management training, and were delighted when in 1990 they averaged 92 hours.*

A series of education and training workshops is needed for people at all levels throughout the organisation – in four broad groups: top management, middle management, first-level supervision and staff. These groups must not, however, be exclusive: often the most successful quality workshops are run with people drawn from all levels in the organisation. This helps to break down barriers and to emphasise the new role of management.

1 *Top management workshop:* the aim of a top management workshop at this point is to secure commitment of the top team to a plan of action to introduce Total Quality. The workshop should contain some theory, but it is essential to emphasise the practical benefits to the organisation. Senior managers will

relate strongly to real information about their own organisation: the results of customer surveys, the cost of quality exercise, and the initiation project meet this need. There is no better way of getting top management's attention than focusing on a substantial prize.

The importance of developing real commitment cannot be underestimated. Workshops alone are rarely enough. Top management need a lot of help: this is the group who can ensure that sufficient resources are provided and properly directed. At this early stage, they will need to:

- understand their role as behavioural role models;
- establish the appropriate organisation for quality;
- understand the tools and techniques of quality improvement, and how they are applied;
- recognise the importance of 'process' and of process capability;
- understand the need to create a climate in which continuous improvement will thrive.

The outputs of the workshop should be:

- commitment of the top team to a specific plan of action to introduce Total Quality;
- the establishment of a Quality Steering Group;
- commitment to a programme of Total Quality awareness training at all levels;
- the identification of corporate priorities for improvement;
- the establishment of challenging goals for improvement.

It is unrealistic to expect instant total commitment. Most top managers start the journey with little knowledge of Total Quality and a degree of scepticism. Why should they be expected to commit their time to an unknown concept?

Table 6 illustrates a typical personal journey to Total Quality. Timescales are very variable, but we have known it take less than a year to move a chief executive from step one to step four. The key is gradually to develop different degrees of commitment, starting with a willingness to learn, followed by an intellectual understanding of the principles. But an intellectual understanding is not enough for managers to commit to behaviour change. That requires an emotional commitment.

2 *Middle management workshop:* these workshops combine an element of theory with a large dose of practical work. Training must be related to the jobs people do. Theory should be restricted to:

- an overview of the structure and foundations of Total Quality;
- leadership, team work and team building;

Table 6 *Steps to commitment*

Step one	Step two	Step three	Step four
Commits time to study the principles.	Intellectually understands the principles.	Emotionally understands the principles.	Acts as a role model for others.
	No real desire to change behaviour.	Works on modifications to own behaviour.	Highly active in encouraging, supporting and coaching people.
	Willing to sponsor pilot improvement projects.	Increases own participation.	Personally and visible highly committed.
	Needs short-term results to maintain commitment.	Fading preoccupation with results, increasing preoccupation with process.	Personally audits the improvement process to identify problem areas.

- applying the most commonly used tools and techniques;
- processes, process capability, measurement and process improvement;
- management behaviour;
- introducing Total Quality – training, organisation, roles, reading, etc.

People learn by doing rather than listening. The main aim of the middle-management workshops should be to help the participants to produce an action plan that they will start to work on immediately. The action plan should be both personal and functional. The functional plan should identify areas of waste and opportunity that the participant will begin to address with his or her people. The action plan should be detailed, specific and not over ambitious. It should include:

- specific opportunities for reducing rework or waste;
- how improvement will be measured;
- what resources will be needed;
- how the improvement projects will be organised;
- what the likely timescales are.

3 *Training for first-level supervision:* supervisors need to be trained in leadership, and in the establishment and maintenance of work standards. Training at this level should also include an understanding of why change to Total

Quality is necessary, the common sense principles, methods of effective communication, and above all, team building. Where appropriate, it should include statistical process control and process capability. The aim should be to equip them to understand how quality can be improved in their own environment, and how to communicate that knowledge to their teams. Topics should include:

- the need for change, and how people are to be involved;
- basic quality principles;
- team leadership role and behaviour;
- characteristics of successful teams;
- dealing with disruptive team behaviour;
- running effective meetings;
- describing problems, collecting and analysing data, and problem-solving;
- overcoming resistance to change;
- holding the gains of improvement.

4 *Training for staff:* staff need training specific to their job, an understanding of what Total Quality is, how it is likely to affect them, and how they will be involved. This training varies greatly depending on the group, but common training topics include:

- the need for change;
- understanding the group's customers and their requirements;
- understanding their suppliers, and working through their requirements with them;
- identifying the business processes they are involved in;
- understanding the effect their own quality can have on others involved in the process;
- identifying areas of waste, rework and errors;
- simple tools and techniques for data collection, analysis and problem solving.

5 *Follow up:* Workshops are just the start of the education and training process. However thorough they are, people will not make progress at the same rate. Follow-up workshops should be held typically three or four months after the first, to allow participants the opportunity to share knowledge, experiences of common barriers to change, difficulties and successes. Peer group support can be harnessed to provide enormous encouragement and help – and recognition. Whereas the first workshop focuses on theory, tools, and behaviour, the second and subsequent workshops at about four-month intervals should be strongly action-oriented.

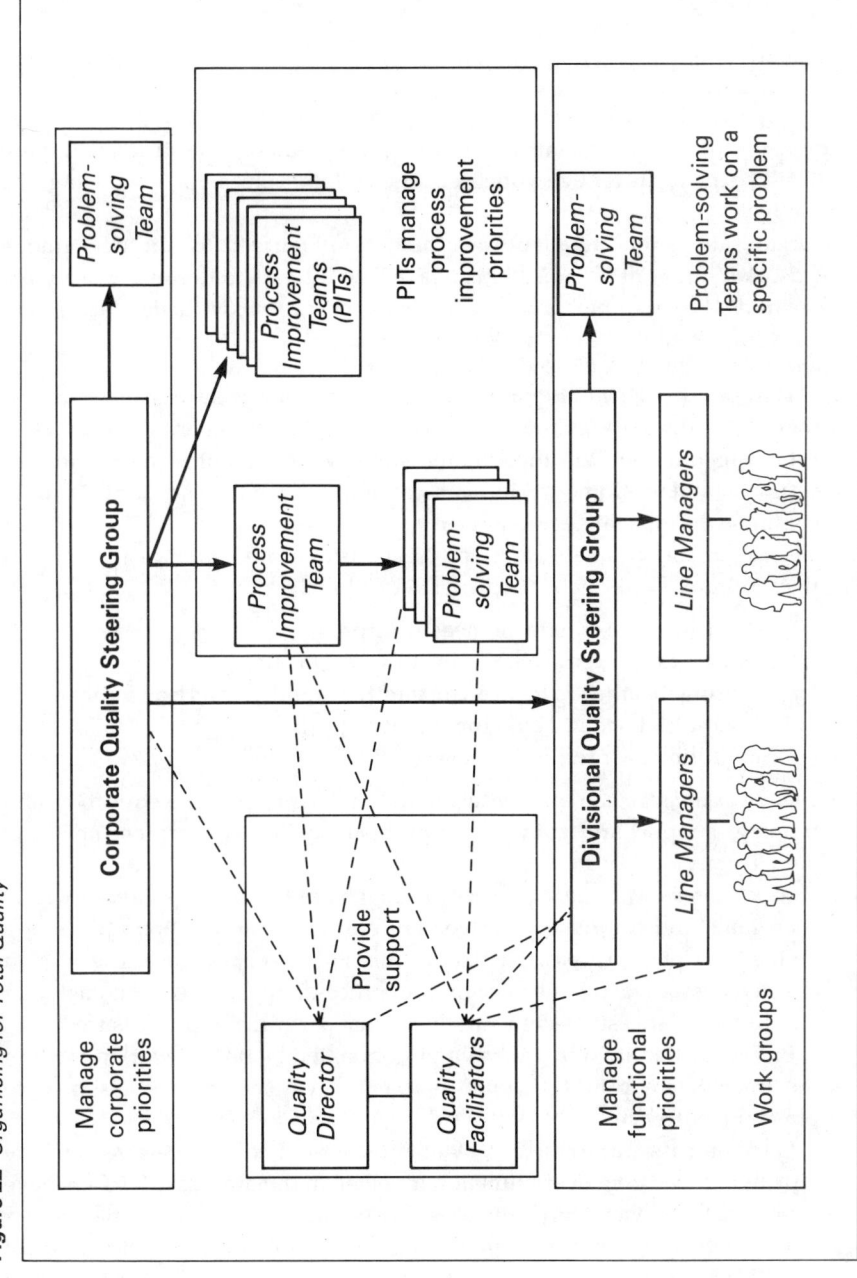

Figure 22 Organising for Total Quality

Organising for quality

Any organisation will need to establish an organisational structure that will guide, encourage and sustain continuous improvement. The structure (Figure 22) will be the focus for everyone's efforts, and the vehicle for 'energising' the initiative.

Organisations tend to adapt the structure in Figure 22 to suit their unique needs, and different organisations use different terms to describe exactly the same thing. For example, problem-solving teams, corrective action teams, and quality improvement teams are synonymous.

1 *Quality steering group:* if quality improvement is to be successful, management must lead the effort. The role of the Quality Steering Group is to establish and monitor the quality strategy and identify and prioritise business and customer objectives for improvement. The group should comprise the top management team.

2 *Quality director:* the quality director's responsibility is to monitor and support the continuous improvement process. This involves:

   (a) establishing the criteria for measuring progress;
   (b) managing the internal marketing of Total Quality;
   (c) ensuring that the top team is constantly reminded of its leadership role;
   (d) providing advice and guidance to managers;
   (e) monitoring the progress of Total Quality.

3 *Quality facilitators:* the quality facilitator's role is to provide education and training, support and guidance to problem-solving and process improvement teams.

4 *Process improvement teams:* process improvement teams (PITs) are formed to coordinate and prioritise improvement efforts within the boundaries of a defined business process. The team's mission is to optimise efficiency and effectiveness of activities within the process, to ensure that customer requirements are established and that actual performance is measured.

   Problems identified by the team or nominated by people working within the process are prioritised and problem-solving teams are assigned to prevent recurrence.

   Each process improvement team must, for it to be effective, include representatives from every function involved in the process. Members have to take a process view rather than their own functional view of problems.

5 *Problem-solving teams:* problem-solving teams are formed to focus on a specific problem. They may be sponsored by the quality steering group, a process improvement team, or a manager. Their aim is to identify the root

cause of the problem, identify the best permanent solution, plan implementation and measure the success of the solution. Usually the team then disbands.

> *A large international manufacturing company established a number of problem-solving teams to test their effectiveness. Within a year, the initial teams had identified savings of $19 million a year. Within two years, over 100 teams were running. Within three years, the number had swollen to 450. Success breeds success!*

6 *Work groups:* work groups are small groups of people who meet voluntarily and regularly to discuss problems in their own work place. They identify problems that affect their output and, where the solution lies within the responsibilities of the group, identify preventive solutions. Where the solution lies outside the group, perhaps in poor quality from an internal supplier, the group's manager is responsible for follow up with those involved.

Stage 3 – Understanding

For an organisation of any size, it seldom takes less than two or three years to reach this stage. There will be evidence of top management commitment to Total Quality, but it may be patchy. Some managers will demonstrate a real understanding of Total Quality, and will have substantially changed their behaviour. Others will be less committed, inconsistent in their behaviour, or even cynical, so that there will be islands of both enthusiasm and cynicism. The emphasis will begin to move from short- to long-term problems. There will be a defined Total Quality process, and the company will be giving off the right external signals to customers and suppliers.

The steps within this stage should include:

- development of a mission statement;
- development of a quality policy;
- internal marketing of quality.

Mission

It may seem odd to leave development of a mission statement to this stage of the process. There is nothing to prevent an organisation doing it earlier, but history suggests that a fair amount of collective experience and genuine change is needed before the exercise becomes relevant. When an organisation is a long way from being able to claim Total Quality as a way of life, mission statements tend to inspire derision.

It is for this reason that mission statements have a bad name. However, there is a huge difference between a mission statement and a sense of mission. A sense of mission provides an inspiring and energising vision for people. It includes both a sense of direction and deeply held values. It provides a focus for action. You do not even need a formal mission statement to have an genuine sense of mission. Some of the most successful companies have never had a formal written mission statement.

The process of developing a mission statement is more important than the end result. It should involve as many people as possible in genuine debate, which itself helps to generate ownership and commitment.

Quality policy

The quality policy provides a foundation on which to build the values and beliefs of the organisation for the future. There is no one right way to articulate a quality policy, but common elements include:

- a statement about products and services;
- a statement for each function, including its relationship with other functions;
- statements for each of the Total Quality foundations.

The quality policy forces top management to think about exactly what quality is to mean for the business. How, for example, will the organisation describe the quality of its products and services in a form that ultimately could be made available to its customers? What does the company expect from its suppliers? What are the responsibilities in relation to quality of finance, marketing, distribution? In terms of leadership, empowerment, and so on, what exactly does the company believe in?

The quality policy poses two questions:

1 What do we want to achieve?
2 How are we going to get there?

As with the mission statement, the benefit of developing a quality policy is that it forces debate at the management level and, ultimately, produces a consensus among the top team of exactly what they mean by quality and how it is to be reflected in products, services, and behaviours. Management should communicate the policy to employees, customers and suppliers, listen carefully to their views, and then make changes that take them into account.

114

Internal marketing of quality

People need to be constantly reminded about the organisation's quality message. There are several ways of marketing quality internally: quality posters, newsletters, videos, systems of recognition, notice boards, visits to customers, quality days, and so forth. This is the 'hype' of Total Quality, and it can be particularly useful at this stage in the transition.

However, great care is needed with hype. If it is done too early, it comes across as exhortation or propaganda, and simply generates cynical resistance. As Mary Walton points out:

> 'Implicit in such sloganeering is the assumption that employees could, if they tried, do better. They are offended, not inspired, by this suggestion. Forced to work with improper or malfunctioning equipment, poor lighting or ventilation, in awkward work spaces under incompetent supervision, they perceive slogans and exhortations as signals that management not only doesn't understand their problems, it doesn't care enough to find out.'[20]

Internal marketing needs to be based on genuine progress. In particular, recognition of teams who have achieved demonstrable success is a powerful motivator that also encourages others. Posters, newsletters and videos need to be genuinely informative and interesting. Visits to customers, especially by groups of people who normally have little or no contact with customers, generate tremendous interest, and are invariably welcomed by the customers.

These things are not just internal marketing, but good practice that should become part of the normal way of doing things. They also remind people to express appreciation of the efforts of others.

As awareness grows and becomes a habit, there is little need for the same intensity of marketing.

Stage 4 – Competence

At this stage, an organisation will have won some important business and cultural advances. Top management will be perceived to be leading and committed to the process. Problem-solving tools and techniques will be in routine use throughout most of the organisation, and the company will have an effective mechanism for aligning people's improvement activities with the overall objectives of the organisation. There will be less preoccupation with results and an increasing emphasis on process.

There will also be a greater emphasis on cross-functional management of processes, team work within and across functions will be greatly improved, and there should be a growing climate of trust and mutual respect between people and management. People will be feeling that they are involved and participating in the business.

Key steps within this stage include:

- cross-functional process management;
- process measurement;
- policy deployment.

Cross-functional process management

In the transition to Total Quality, the need for cross-functional cooperation becomes apparent at the earliest stages, and a great deal of progress can be made within a functional organisation to encourage it. However, it is not until most of the barriers that we described in Chapter 6 have been broken down that an organisation can move to genuine process management.

Process measurement (which we discuss below) must replace functionally oriented measures. Functional ownership and 'accountability' has to be replaced by process ownership.

Each key process within the organisation must have a *process owner* – the individual most appropriate to guide changes to the process across functional boundaries. Process ownership cuts across functional reporting lines: this simply will not happen until those reporting lines are weakened. They should not be *broken* – they must become lines of professional and technical support, and as such, no longer a barrier to change.

The process owner leads a process improvement team, which has representatives from every function involved in the process. The duties of a process improvement team are to:

- consider improvement proposals received from staff;
- define priorities for improvement;
- assign projects to problem-solving teams;
- approve proposed changes to the process;
- coordinate the planning of changes to the process;
- measure the improving efficiency and effectiveness of the process;
- communicate the results.

Process measurement

The process improvement team is responsible for the definition of Key Process Indicators (KPIs). KPIs are permanent measures of the effectiveness and efficiency of the process. At key points in the process – sometimes called 'pulse points' – they measure throughput volumes alongside factors such as:

- Frequency of occurrence;
- Accuracy or error rates;
- Completeness;
- Timeliness;
- Speed of response;

which have a useful acronym – FACTS.

Why measure? Simply, without measurement there is seldom much prospect of finding out what is happening, and no prospect of lasting improvement.

> In a clearing bank, irritated customers complaining about the number of cashpoint machines that were out of action prompted the bank, for the first time, to measure their availability. It was found to be unacceptably low, averaging 92 per cent. Delivery of the cashpoint service was recognised as a cross-functional process with a complex web of interdependencies involving the machines themselves, branch control computers, the telecommunications network, the computer centre, links to reciprocal banks and their computers, all of which could and did fail from time to time. Furthermore, it involved branch staff who had to fill the machines with notes, security transport who had to deliver them, the cash centres who had to sort the notes, computer operators, software developers, suppliers of the machines, and so on. A variety of problems emerged, including failure to stock the machines at the right times, jams in the note feed mechanism, computer and network breakdowns.
>
> The bank started a relentless process of collecting data at different points in the process to identify the frequency of each type of problem. It found, for example, that the most common problem was jams in the note feed mechanism. This in turn was affected by the quality and age of the notes. It was uneconomic to use only new notes, and in the short term it was cost-effective to employ an army of Sunday temporary staff to unfold notes with their corners turned down and iron them flat! Meantime the bank worked with its cashpoint machine suppliers to improve the feed mechanism, and then moved on to tackle the other problems. Each involved different

functions cooperating to improve the process. Machine availability improved steadily and customer complaints declined.

Policy deployment

The entire premise of policy deployment is that the people who are charged with executing a plan must participate in the planning process. The benefits of participation come from the belief that people *want* to do the right things. How can they know what is right if they are not permitted to participate in the process by which overall priorities are set? Lacking that insight, functions will tend to develop a view of what is right for their function, which may not necessarily be what is best for the business overall.

Policy deployment is the backbone of Total Quality – the vertical element. It is inextricably linked with cross-functional process management, which is the horizontal element, rather in the way that fabric has a warp and a weft, the vertical and horizontal threads. Both are needed to give it substance.

Policy deployment starts with the key themes or core business objectives that top management determines to pursue. By a top-down, iterative process which the Japanese call 'catchball', managers negotiate their own functional goals based around the key themes. Once these have been accepted by senior management, they develop detailed implementation plans – the means by which the goals will be achieved – and precise numerical measures to track progress. Progress is monitored and each month the plan is updated in line with actual progress. Flexibility and the ability to adapt the plan in response to business changes is critical.

Policy deployment also applies at the continuous improvement level. Improvement opportunities can be prioritised in terms of their impact on the functional targets so that the drive for continuous improvement is steered in the most effective direction to meet the key objectives of the business.

The main difference between policy deployment and traditional planning systems such as management by objectives, is the highly participative nature of the way in which goals are set, and the emphasis placed on the means by which the goals are achieved.

Stage 5 – Deep understanding

By now, a culture of participative leadership will exist at all levels and everyone will be involved in quality improvement in some shape or form. Management will be behaving as role models and making themselves visible and accessible to everyone. They will be involved in building awareness of Total Quality and in reviewing progress. The importance of recognition as a prime motivator will be well developed.

Total Quality principles will have guided the development of the organisation's mission, strategy, values and beliefs, and these will have been communicated across the whole organisation. Its strategic planning will be based on sound data – including customer feedback, benchmarking and other competitive data. The relevance of the strategy and its effectiveness will be kept under constant review.

Processes will be managed across functional boundaries and the barriers between functions will have been replaced by a mutual understanding of the requirements of internal supplier/customer relationships. Process improvement will be continual, and well aligned with the organisation's overall business objectives. Process measurement techniques will be routine.

The organisation will not be just satisfying customers, it will be regularly delighting them.

This kind of company is a potential quality award winner. It is unlikely that a company will reach this stage in less than five years of starting a Total Quality process.

Quality awards

Japan has the 'Deming prize'. Like the Hollywood Oscars, the Deming award ceremony is broadcast on prime time television. For Japanese companies, the award is highly prestigious. In the USA, the 'Malcolm Baldrige' award is attracting similar interest. In Europe the first 'European Quality Award' (EQA) was won by Rank Xerox in 1992.

For most companies that enter, perhaps the real value of applying for an award is not the winning of it, but the opportunity to benchmark the organisation against world class quality management criteria, to identify areas of improvement. Pride is also a powerful factor, and a very positive driver of behaviour.

Stage 6 – World class

World class does not mean large or supremely profitable. Non-profit organisations can be world class. We prefer the notion that a world class organisation has four fundamental characteristics:

1 *Staying power:* a company's external image sometimes flatters reality. What we have described as the barriers to Total Quality are extremely powerful

forces, and complacency following partial success is pride's mistress. Total Quality should ultimately be a self-perpetuating obsession with improvement.

2 *Learning:* adaptability is profoundly important: the whole organisation may need to make radical shifts in its positioning and capability in order to respond to external changes in its environment. A 'learning organisation' will be capable of such changes to its core technologies, organisation, skill base, products and services.

3 *Creativity:* this is not simply that an organisation attracts and nourishes creative individuals, but that their very association sparks innovation, lateral thought and risk taking. This implies the complete absence of internal barriers.

4 *Morality:* the organisation, what it stands for, its internal and external relationships and its place in the outside world should constitute a force for good.

Such companies will be the models that others will strive to emulate – and the proof that there is always something better to aim at.

Roland E. Magnin, Executive Vice President of the Xerox Corporation,[21] has said:

> 'We've come to the conclusion that while quality is critical to our continued survival, it alone will not be enough to enable us to truly succeed, to win, to meet our goals.

> 'Why is that so? First is the question of our competitors. Our major competitors – the Japanese – are very strong in quality also. While we think we're pretty good at quality improvement, the reality is that we will, at best, maintain parity with the Japanese. It will not create a large enough lead to be a sustainable competitive advantage for us.'

He went on to describe Xerox's first steps in the design of radically different organisation structures, in using what he sees as Western cultural strengths to develop competitive advantage, and in using the corporation's own knowledge and capabilities in document management to offer its customers competitive advantage.

A powerful illustration of world class capability is given in a recent study[22] led by Daniel Jones, Professor of Industry Management at Cardiff Business School. Some of the results are given in Table 7.

The study compared productivity and quality standards achieved by Japanese and UK automotive component suppliers. It examined 18 companies,

Table 7 *Benchmarking Project: Automotive Component Suppliers*

	World class	Other
Productivity index (units per hour)	95.0	53.7
Quality (defects)	0.025%	2.5%
Space utilisation index*	89.4	64.4
Throughput time index*	59.1	32.4
Operations automated	46%	32%
Rework and rectification	1.5%	4.1%
Stock turnover ratio (per year)	93.6	32.4
Employees in problem solving	80%	54%
Schedule variability	5.5%	11.9%
Source: Lean Production Benchmarking Project		* 100 × best

nine in Japan and nine in the UK. The top third were all Japanese, and while not all Japanese companies were uniformly capable, the five worst performers were British.

The automotive industry in the UK has been one of the pioneer sectors in Total Quality, and has made enormous progress. World-class companies have nevertheless developed an awesome capability.

We have much still to do.

CHAPTER 8

Pitfalls

'Survival is not compulsory'

Dr W. Edwards Deming

Since the late 1970s, thousands of organisations have launched quality improvement initiatives. There have been spectacular successes:

1 Hewlett-Packard has cut the time it takes to develop a printer from 53 months to 22 months, and now aims to reduce this further to 12 months. Just one improvement project yielded $50 million in savings. Product failures are down 60 per cent. Productivity is up 90 per cent. Market share has doubled!
2 3M has reduced justified customer complains by almost 70 per cent.
3 British Airways achieved a reduction 'beyond their wildest dreams' in engineering costs in a single year, and attributes much of the credit for its 20 per cent growth in passenger traffic during the mid-1980s to its 'Putting People First' programme.
4 Mitel Semiconductors achieved an 80 per cent reduction in development cycle time.
5 Land Rover took the Discovery from drawing board to showroom in less than three years – a 50 per cent reduction over earlier models, and a world class benchmark.

Unfortunately it is also true that many organisations have been disappointed by the progress they have made. Success, or the lack of it, is of course a comparative term. We doubt whether any company that has launched a quality improvement programme will have failed to win some real improvements. But success is always measured against expectations and dramatic success stories create high expectations.

Companies usually start their Total Quality initiatives by building awareness of quality issues, training people, establishing improvement teams, and so on.

Managers go to conferences, watch video tapes, and attend workshops. Other organisations are visited, facilitators are trained, and so on. In spite of all of these things, people fail to become enthusiastic advocates, quality projects drag into infinity, the transformation in performance that management wanted does not transpire. Where is the big payoff that management expected?

It is tempting to think of quality improvement in the same terms as dieting. People who successfully hold the gains of weight reduction do not do so through short-term diets, visits to health farms, or exercise. They do it by making fundamental changes to their lifestyle. Similarly, tools and techniques will not make Total Quality successful. The difference between success and failure is a fundamental change in management behaviour.

Pitfalls in the transition to Total Quality

Our experience and research have led us to define eleven key pitfalls in the transition to Total Quality:

1 lack of management commitment;
2 lack of vision and direction;
3 excessive inward focus;
4 measurement paralysis;
5 technical focus;
6 compromising quality;
7 people not really involved;
8 quick fix mentality;
9 quality remains a separate activity;
10 lack of quality definitions;
11 Total Quality as a mandatory religion

Lack of management commitment

Commitment is more than a word. Any manager will say that he or she is committed to quality, but actions do not always live up to words.

> *A director wrote a memo to his direct reports asking for their comments on a complex issue within three days. The reaction was very negative. Part of the problem was the very short timescale. But this was not the real problem. The memo concluded with the sentence '— not that I ever listen to your comments anyway!'.*

A Scot with a sardonic sense of humour, he was genuinely committed to quality improvement. Unfortunately the context removed the intended humour and was taken at face value. He drew a serious conclusion from their reaction: particularly at times of major change and uncertainty, people's sensitivities make it important for management to be aware of the signals they put out.

Unless management's actions are consistent with their messages, no one is going to be convinced that they are serious. In Chapter 5, we described a role model for managers in a Total Quality environment, to help understand how commitment can be translated into behaviour.

Some symptoms of lack of management commitment:

- *Misuse of Total Quality:* a UK insurance company started Total Quality, but six months later announced a programme of redundancies. People linked these to Total Quality, and cooperation ended immediately.
- *Management are spectators, not participants:* preaching the importance of continuous improvement is not enough. In fact preaching alone will inspire nothing more than cynicism. There has to be substance. Management must be *involved:* in improvement teams; in improving their own management processes; in improving communications; in recognising achievement. Management can bring energy and life to Total Quality. Equally their lack of participation can drain the life away. Their active participation is the key to both success and failure.
- *Management do not believe they are the cause of the problem:* if managers persist in believing that employees are the cause of the problem, virtually no progress will be made. Management are 95 per cent of the problem and have 95 per cent of the authority to win improvements. It is management's job to ensure that people have the right training, equipment, support and resources to do a quality job. If managers at least start with the assumption that they are the cause of the problem, in the unlikely event that they turn out to be wrong, it will come as a pleasant surprise.
- *Management do not make Total Quality part of the organisation fabric:* Total Quality is not a separate activity, it is the way of managing the business. If continuous improvement is not linked to the organisation's overall objectives, people will inevitably view it as a short-term programme, not a long-term strategic commitment.
- *Management do not 'energise' Total Quality:* Total Quality is very hard work. It needs constant reinforcement and encouragement to bring it to life and to sustain momentum. Without reinforcement, Total Quality will become tepid. The key energisers are: recognition, leadership, internal marketing

and education and training. Management need to keep these 'energisers' fully deployed at all stages of Total Quality.

Lack of vision and direction

Many organisations' quality initiatives appear to be 'going nowhere in particular'. People need to see that the organisation is following a rational strategy – focused on appropriate objectives, needs and capabilities.

Lacking direction, the danger is that groups and functions will – in good faith – set their own functional objectives. These may or may not be aligned with corporate objectives. In the early stages of quality improvement, some fragmentation and parochialism is inevitable. But as an organisation gains experience, the need to align quality objectives and business objectives becomes more important. Chapter 2 on positioning and capability, and the discussion on policy deployment in Chapter 7 describe the means by which quality and business objectives can be aligned.

Excessive inward focus

Many organisations focus only on improvements to internal efficiency. The prime focus of Total Quality should be meeting customer needs, not productivity enhancement. If people believe that 'efficiency' is the prime objective, fear may remain a major obstacle.

Measurement paralysis

Measurement of improvement is critical: without measurement, there is no evidence of improvement and there is no anchor by which to hold the gains. There is growing evidence that the organisations most successful in introducing Total Quality (measured by the results they have achieved) emphasise strongly the need for tangible results in their improvement efforts.

However, some organisations go to extremes. There is a probably apocryphal story of an organisation where visitors would always be impressed by the number of charts on walls throughout the whole building. They were less impressed by the employee whose chart recorded the number of times he was asked what his chart was measuring.

There are two types of measures: Key Process Indicators (KPIs) and Improvement Measures. A small number of KPIs should provide *permanent* measures of continuous process improvement. They are systematically collected and are widely circulated around the organisation. Improvement measures demonstrate the effects of a specific process improvement. They are temporary. The need for them ceases to exist when a solution to a problem has been proven successful.

Excessive measurement dilutes effort and confuses.

Technical focus

Tools and techniques are important, but they should not be allowed to obscure the need for behavioural change. There is no doubt that to build a climate of prevention, you have to use tools. But, some organisations become so enamoured with tools that they lose sight of the real objectives – the continuous improvement of products and services.

Compromising quality

No organisation can have a credible quality improvement process if its managers daily make decisions that compromise quality.

> In a manufacturing company, if monthly orders were poor, managers were sometimes instructed to ship products ahead of schedule to boost that month's statistics – thereby compromising customer needs for JIT delivery.

> In a semiconductor manufacturing company, new products were initially manufactured in Europe or the USA – both high labour cost areas. As processes became robust, they were transferred to low labour cost plants in Asia. But the company was reluctant to transfer knowledge from one plant to another for cost reasons. As a result, quality was compromised while the new plant went through a learning curve.

> Again in the same company, salesmen were organised along product stream lines. To meet their own sales targets, they would sometimes sell products from their own stream even if a product from a rival stream would better meet customer needs.

From a top management perspective, this is the toughest of all the pitfalls. Faced with short-term objectives – sales targets, meeting budget, and so forth – the pressure to meet targets at the expense of longer-term objectives is very difficult to resist. From a middle-management perspective, having to compromise quality makes a nonsense of everything Total Quality stands for. This is an area where top management really need to bite the bullet, since the decision not to compromise quality may have a painful short-term impact on business results.

> *The CEO of a European car manufacturer delayed the launch of a critical new model just before an eagerly awaited launch date. He explained that he was not convinced that the company would be able to produce a consistently high level of quality, and he would not allow the launch to proceed as planned until the quality problems had been resolved.*

People not really involved

It is easy to build the infrastructure of continuous improvement: quality steering groups, problem-solving teams, and so on – but these only involve a small fraction of the people, and not at the grass roots level. To mobilise the total workforce, everyone has to be involved. Education and training, skills development, small group activities and suggestion schemes are all vehicles for securing grass roots involvement.

Quick fix mentality

The creditable desire to do something to improve customer service or product quality is too often translated into the discreditable action of doing something quickly. Quality improvement does require patience. While there is nothing wrong with a sense of urgency, management's impatience too often leads to short cuts, which in turn leads to a failure to address root causes and to find the best solution to a problem.

Quality remains a separate activity

Particularly in the initial stages, there is need for a quality organisation: a quality director and quality facilitators, problem-solving teams, process owners, and so on. The danger is that this resource is perceived to be responsible for quality. As a result, quality problems can all too easily be 'thrown over the wall' to the quality people rather than being dealt with by line managers.

Lack of quality definitions

Organisations need to be very clear about what they mean by quality. Without guidance, functions need little encouragement to find enhancements to the service they provide to their internal customers, irrespective of need or the cost of providing those enhancements.

While delighting customers is a legitimate objective in relation to external customers, delighting internal customers needs to be carefully balanced against its cost.

Total Quality as a mandatory religion

Sometimes, top management undergo something akin to a religious experience in converting to Total Quality. They see the light and suddenly become born-again quality converts, zealously expounding their new beliefs and demonstrating intolerance of others who may not be quite so far down the road to Damascus.

Not everyone converts quite so easily. People prefer to have a clear vision of where Total Quality is taking them, how they are going to be involved, and how it is going to affect them. Without it, Total Quality can be seen as threatening, or the flavour of the month.

The two-year cycle

It is not uncommon to find that the initial enthusiasm for Total Quality starts to decline after a period of 12 to 24 months. One reason is that management can easily become satisfied that the real achievements their organisation has won are good enough. As soon as their eye comes off the ball, the benefits will start to slip away. As soon as employees become content with their efforts, they stop improving. Employees and management alike must share a common belief that they can always do better.

It is also possible to sustain an improvement effort for a period of time without tackling the barriers described in Chapter 6 – performance appraisal, management by results, and so forth. But if they are allowed to continue to drive management behaviour they will stop transition in its tracks.

> At a UK plastics manufacturer, office staff parked their cars at the front of the building – shop floor staff had to park at the back; the office got free coffee – the shop floor had to pay; the office had flexitime, the shop floor clocked in; there were three restaurants – blue collar, white collar and management, with different quality of food.
>
> In a life assurance company, salesmen were appraised on a 1 to 5 basis. 'Fives' were star performers, and were given annual trips to the Caribbean. What

incentive was there for the stars to share the secrets of their success with their less successful colleagues? Would that not compromise their ability to be a star performer next year? Surely what the company really needed was a team in which everyone was a star performer.

In an industrial laundry, garments moved down a mechanised rail to a packing station. Every few minutes, a garment fell off the rail onto the dirty floor. An operator only a few feet away studiously ignored a steadily accumulating pile of dirty garments just out of his reach. He was on piecework. To pick the garments up, he would have to stop packing – thereby directly affecting his pay.

Even when the barriers have been eliminated, it is common for enthusiasm to wane. A successful Total Quality process requires constant reinforcement through communication, education and training, recognition and internal marketing. Occasionally, it needs a shot of adrenalin.

A manufacturing company acquired a competitor, which provided an opportunity for many of its managers and staff to become involved in establishing a quality drive in the new subsidiary.

Such cycles are a normal part of a Total Quality process. The key is to recognise when the process is losing momentum, and to take action to revitalise it.

CHAPTER 9

Noblesse oblige

'Noblesse oblige . . . rank imposes obligations.'

Chambers English Dictionary

Ultimately, only two things differentiate one company from another: the first is the ability of people to work together to delight customers; the other is leadership.

People have little difficulty in recognising the value of both. We all derive pleasure from constructive association with other people, and prefer cooperation to conflict. Leadership is the critical factor in whether such cooperation exists.

Leadership can be learnt. This book is fundamentally concerned with the role of management at all levels, and in every functional discipline. Every functional head is first and foremost a manager – a *leader* – whose most important characteristic is the ability to foster teamwork and develop the capabilities of others.

Total Quality is a system of behaviour that nurtures both leadership and teamwork. Managers have positions of authority not as a reward, but because they have an obligation to the staff that work with them: *noblesse oblige* brought up to date.

The enterprises that survive and prosper into the next century will be those that harness the talents of all their people to create and deliver value, and that can sustain that culture.

Notes

1 *The Effectiveness of Quality Improvement in British Business*, Develin & Partners, 1988.
2 Philip B.Crosby, *Quality Is Free*, McGraw-Hill, 1979.
3 See note 2.
4 Extracted from Masaaki Imai, *Kaizen*, McGraw-Hill, 1986.
5 Dr W. Edwards Deming, *Out of the Crisis*, Massachusetts Institute of Technology, Center for Advanced Engineering Study, 1986; Cambridge University Press, 1988.
6 Mal Owen, *SPC and Continuous Improvement*, IFS Publications, 1989.
7 Organisational classification developed in conjunction with M2i-Stratorg, the French management consultancy.
8 Technical Assistance Research Program, USA, 1988.
9 Reprinted from Shelley Berman, *A Hotel is a Funny Place*, with permission from Price Stern Sloan, Inc., Los Angeles, CA., USA, 1972, 1985.
10 See note 1.
11 Developed in conjunction with Murray Duffin, Vice President, Service and Quality, SGS-Thomson Micrelectronics.
12 See note 1.
13 Joint NASS/JHRA survey, USA, 1988.
14 *Quality: Focusing on Productivity and People for Enhanced Competitive Advantage*, presentation by Roland E. Magnin, Executive Vice President, of the Xerox Corporation at The Global Quality Management Conference, Brussels, Belgium, 27 October 1992.
15 Frederick Herzberg, 'One More Time: How Do You Motivate Employees?', *Harvard Business Review*, September–October 1987.
16 Rafael Aguayo, *Dr Deming: The Man who Taught the Japanese about Quality*, Mercury Books, 1991.
17 See note 5.
18 H. Johnson and Robert S. Kaplan, *Relevance Lost: the Rise and Fall of Management Accounting*, Harvard Business School Press, 1987.

19 For more information see Robin Bellis-Jones and Nick Develin, Accountants Digest No. 281, *Activity Based Cost Management*, Accountancy Books, 1992.

20 Mary Walton, *The Deming Management Method*, Dodd, Mead & Co, 1986; Mercury Books 1991.

21 See note 14.

22 The Enterprise Benchmarking Project, reported in the *Financial Times*, 8 January 1993.

23 See note 1.

Quality improvement tools and techniques

'For every problem, there is a solution that is neat, plausible, and wrong.'

H. L. Mencken

Under pressure and often with more than one problem to solve, most managers use experience, intuition and gut feel to find solutions. Often the problem reappears after a time, or surfaces in a slightly different form, or even becomes more serious. What appears to be a solution will be ineffective unless it addresses the root cause of the problem.

Although fire fighting is sometimes necessary even in quality award-winning companies, Total Quality seeks to introduce a structure and discipline into problem solving. By collecting data to identify a problem and to isolate its root causes, by working through several alternative solutions to identify the best, and by collecting more data to prove the efficacy of the solution, problems can be prevented from recurring.

This appendix gives a brief overview of the basic tools and techniques, and of a structured and disciplined approach to problem solving. It is beyond the scope of this book to describe these tools and techniques in detail. They range from simple and basic tools that everyone can use, such as pareto charts and cause and effect (Ishikawa) diagrams, to very complex tools that require extensive knowledge and experience, such as Quality Function Deployment, and Taguchi's design of experiments. There is a great deal of published material on the tools and techniques of Total Quality, and we have included a number of useful sources in Appendix C.

Basic tools and techniques

The following illustrate the basic tools and techniques that can be used to assist with problem solving.

Figure 23 Fishbone (Ishikawa) diagram

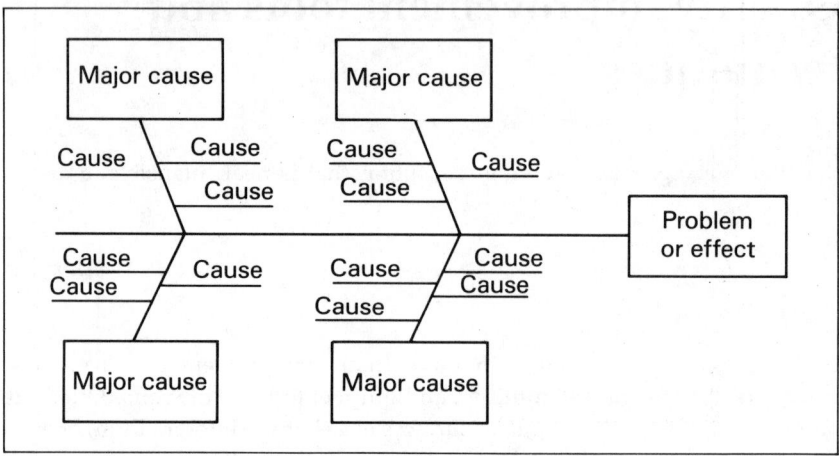

Fishbone diagrams, often called Ishikawa diagrams after their inventor, show cause and effect. They are particularly useful in facilitating brainstorming sessions with a group of people. Their main purpose is to tap the knowledge of the group about the current causes of a problem, so that improvements can be made by preventing or eliminating them. Main causes can be generic headings such as 'methods', 'materials', 'machinery', 'manpower' and 'measurements' – known as the 'Five Ms'. A 'reverse Ishikawa diagram' is useful when evaluating solutions to problems and planning implementation: the solution is placed in a box on the left of the chart, and the effects of the solution are added to the branches of the fishbone.

Figure 24 Pareto analysis

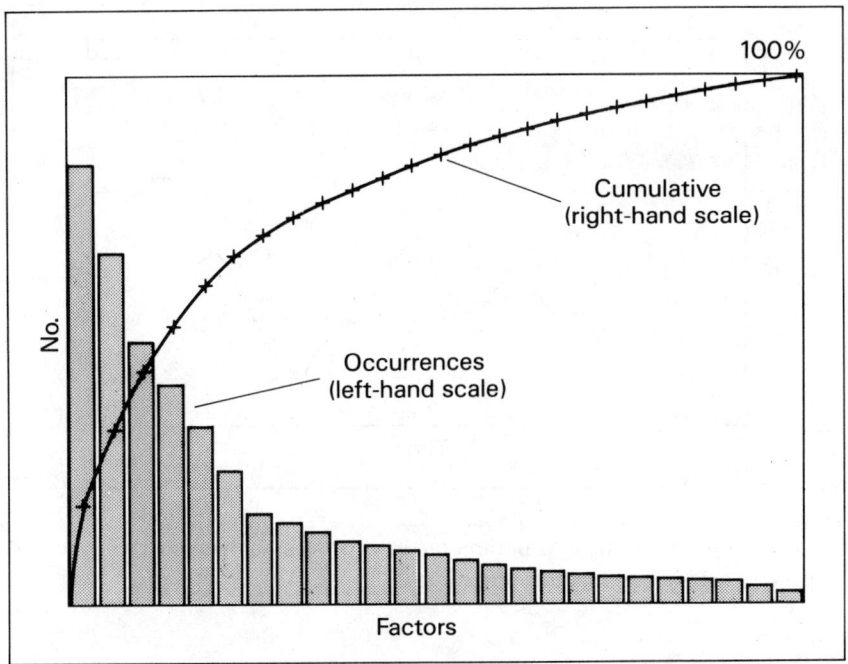

Pareto analyses are bar charts that show different factors in descending sequence of their occurrence. Their purpose is to separate out the 'vital few' from the trivial many (the '80/20 rule'), and thereby to help prioritise action to make improvements.

Figure 25 Run chart

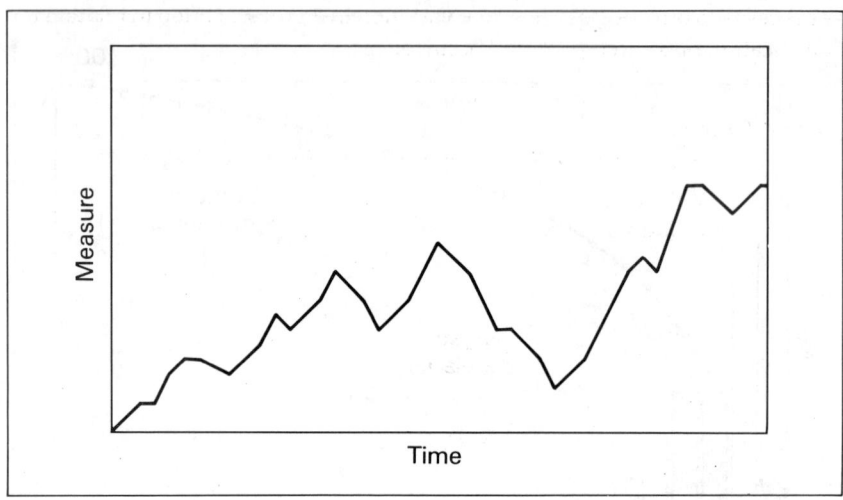

A *run chart* shows how a parameter in a process behaves over time. Its purpose is to hightlight trends and cycles.

Figure 26 Histogram

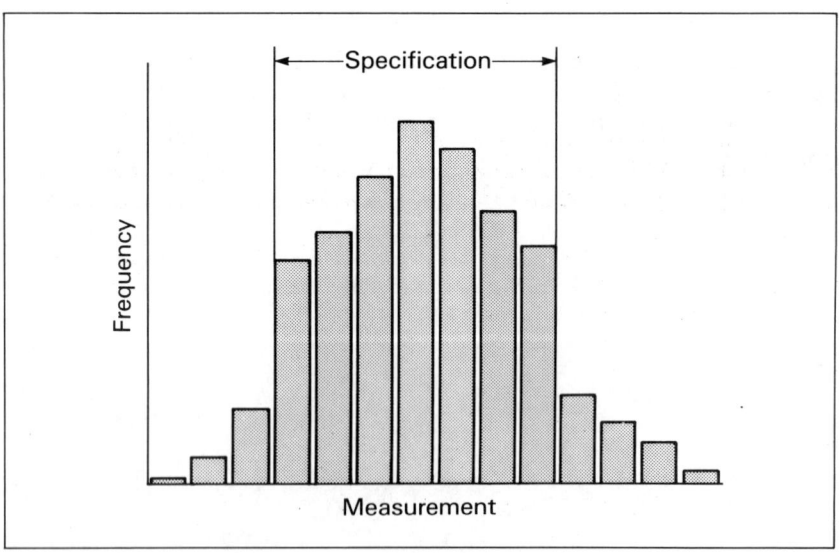

A *histogram* shows the frequency of occurrence of a measured characteristic of a process. Its purpose is to describe variation in a process, often in relation to a specification or desired profile of occurrences.

Figure 27 Scatter diagram

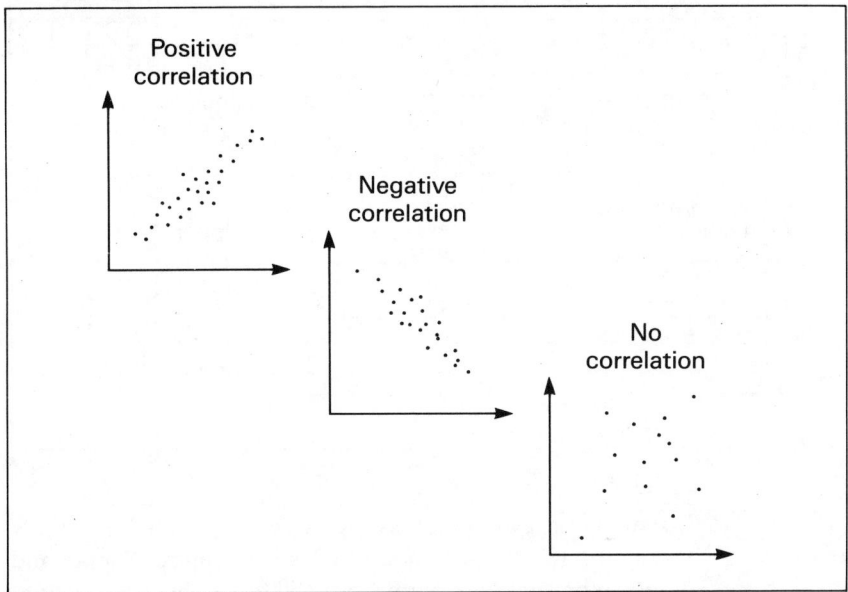

A *scatter diagram* shows the relationship between two variables. Its purpose is to establish whether there exists a correlation between the two variables, and is particularly useful in identifying relationships between causes and effects.

Figure 28 Control chart

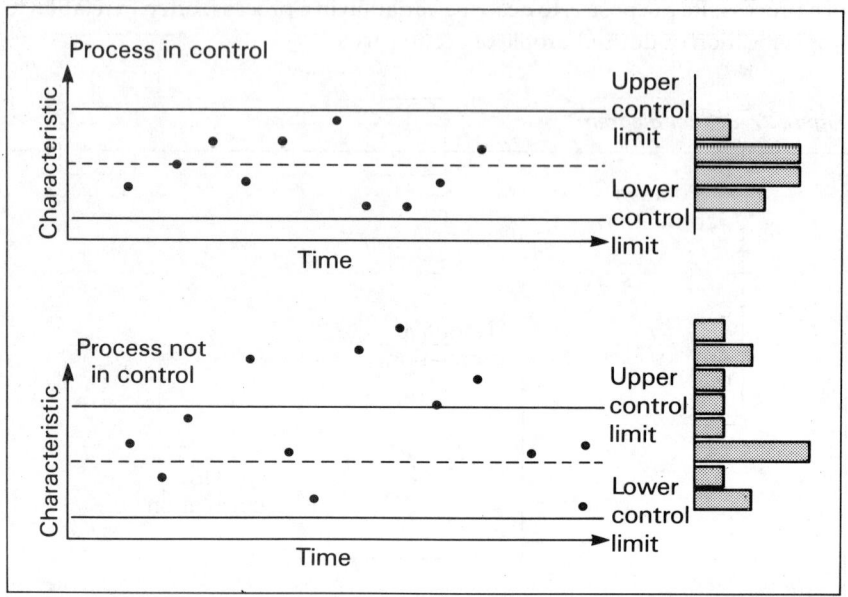

A *control chart* shows a measured process characteristic sampled over time. Its purpose is to identify whether or not a process is in control. Upper and lower control limits represent the normal capability of the process (not specification limits). Occurrences outside the control limits indicate special causes of variation against which the process is not robust. A histogram can be drawn from the chart data.

Figure 29 Flow chart

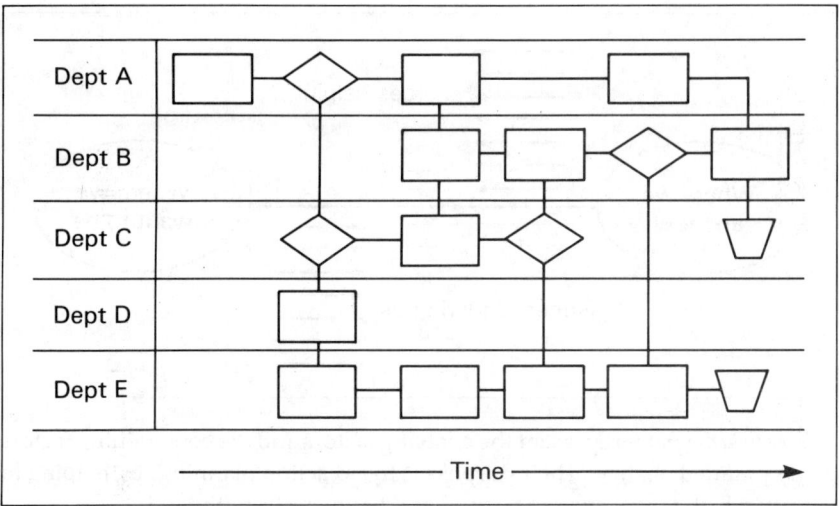

A *flow chart* is a visual representation of the steps in a process. Its purpose is to show the links between activities, the source of inputs and the destination of outputs. Flow charts are particularly useful in highlighting participating groups, decision points, rework loops, and time delays, and help track back to the root causes of process failures.

Figure 30 Force field diagram

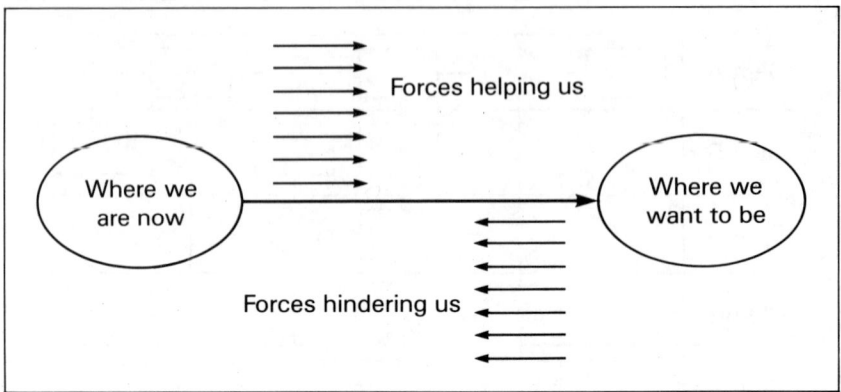

Force field diagrams represent the enabling factors and the constraining factors in any planned change. Their purpose is to aid action planning, by helping to identify which forces need to be weakened, which strengthened.

Figure 31 Activity analysis

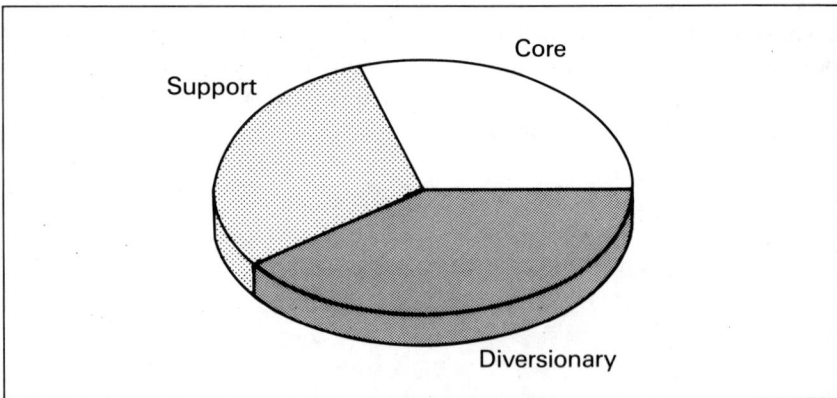

Activity analysis is described in Chapter 7. Its purpose is to identify which activities in a process add value, and which do not, in order to focus attention on the causes of diversionary activity, on opportunities to leverage core activity, and on activities which would benefit from methods improvement. Activity analysis is particularly useful when used in conjunction with process maps (flow charts) to help track back to root causes of diversionary activity, and in process redesign.

Table 8 *The continuous improvement cycle*

Step	Typical activities	Tools	Outputs
1 – Define the problem and organise the team	Complete problem definition Schedule team activities	Brainstorming Data collection Interviews Who, what, where, when, why, how, how many? ('5W2H')	Problem definition Team mission Timescales
2 – Identify outputs and customers' expectations	Identify outputs and customers Identify customers' requirements Establish measures and collect data Assess conformance to requirements Identify deficiencies	Interviews Flowcharts Customer needs surveys	List of outputs/products and services provided to customers Customer requirements and satisfaction analysis Gap analyses
3 – Describe the current process	Identify inputs and suppliers Flowchart the process or sub-process Collect data Establish goals for improvement Collect data	Flowcharts (process maps) Activity data collection	List of inputs and suppliers Process maps Activity analysis (core, support, diversionary) Improvement goals and measurement criteria
4 – Identify root causes	Analyse data Brainstorm Identify 'vital few' root causes	Fishbone diagrams Pareto diagrams Histograms Run charts Scatter diagrams	List of root causes to be addressed by the solution
5 – Find the best solution	Develop potential solutions Test effects Select best solution(s)	Solution effect diagrams (reverse Ishikawa) Force field diagrams	Description of best solution(s)

Table 8—continued

Step	Typical activities	Tools	Outputs
6 – Implement	Plan implementation Identify verification data and collection methods Identify standards, measures, training, and documentation requirements Identify preventive/contingency actions Communicate/discuss with those affected by the change	Action plan – events, timing, training, communications Run charts Key Process Indicators Improvement measures	Implemented solution(s)
7 – Verify the solution	Monitor and measure solution effect and action plan	Action plan Run charts Improvement measures	Measured effect of the solution
8 – Hold the gains	Identify areas for replication Modify standards and targets Identify measures, method and frequency	Action plan Key Process Indicators Improvement measures	Recommended actions to hold the gains Monitoring measures New goals
9 – Celebrate success	Review team performance Recognise success.	Brainstorming Team review	Recommended improvements to the continuous improvement cycle
10 – Start again			

The continuous improvement cycle

Most problems are best solved by a team, because it brings more minds to bear on the problem and, by involving those affected by the solution, it secures their commitment to implementation. The continuous improvement cycle is a team-based, structured approach to problem solving. Table 8 illustrates the steps in the cycle, typical activities carried out, tools used and deliverables of each step.

It may appear at first sight that the approach is rigid and inflexible. It is not meant to be. There are times when the approach can be shortened by eliminating steps, but this ought to be the exception. The approach is designed to identify the root causes of a problem, the best solution, the best means of implementation, and the best way of holding on to the gains.

The importance of tools and techniques

The true values of tools and techniques, and of a structured approach to problem solving depends on the extent to which they become routine within the organisation. Without them, good ideas are wasted through poor implementation; bad ideas go unchallenged. Initiative for change depends on gut feel and instinct, and therefore becomes personal and individual – not cooperative.

When all staff, at all levels, are thoroughly trained in their use, they play a significant role in reinforcing and supporting the behavioural and structural elements of Total Quality.

BS 5750 and equivalent standards

Most organisations – industrial, commercial or governmental – produce a product or service intended to satisfy a customer's requirements. Such requirements are often incorporated in a 'specification' describing acceptable quality characteristics. Technical specifications do not however ensure that the customers' needs are consistently met, nor do they necessarily reflect exactly what the customers' requirements really are. If the specification or business process is deficient, products and services will equally be deficient. Consequently, this has led to the development of quality system standards and guidelines that complement the technical requirements provided in a technical specification.

In the UK, these standards are embodied in BS 5750 which is directly equivalent to the series of International Standards ISO 9000 to ISO 9004 inclusive. The quality system of an organisation is influenced by its objectives, by the nature of the product or service it produces, and by the procedures specific to the organisation. Therefore, the quality system varies from one organisation to another.

BS 5750 was first published in 1979, and over 9000 organisations have been assessed and registered against it, or a directly equivalent standard such as the Defence AQAP series of standards.

Advantages of BS 5750

BS 5750 brings a number of potential advantages to an organisation:

- *Policy:* it forces an organisation to determine its policies and objectives and communicate them to its staff.
- *Procedures:* it makes an organisation put in place documented procedures to cover a range of issues including: procedures for the activities by which service is provided; checking that specified service levels are being achieved;

undertaking and receiving contracts with suppliers; controlling documents; and taking corrective action to overcome problems. Commendably, the standard for a quality system extends through planning, production and service to encompass design, purchasing, process development, inspection and test, packing and storage, sales and distribution, installation and operation, technical assurance and maintenance, and marketing.

Having to document procedures helps people focus on deciding how these things really ought to be done and helps to create a discipline to follow the procedure. It can also help to identify training needs.

- *Customer requirements:* the number of industries and customers that require their suppliers to be registered is rapidly increasing. In some industries, such as the motor industry, registration is a *minimum* requirement.
- *Publicity:* some organisations can obtain good publicity from registration, particularly if they can beat their competitors to registration.
- *Morale:* registration is a reason for people to be able to take a little more pride in their work and in the organisation. It means something to be part of a quality accredited organisation.
- *A help to overall quality improvement*: our survey[23] found that fewer companies registered against BS 5750 reported poor results from their quality improvement efforts that those who were not registered, although a definite cause and effect relationship was not established. It may just be that companies registering against BS 5750 simply have a higher level of commitment that those who do not. It is also likely that they are more aware of their customers' needs, particularly if the customers require accreditation.

Shortcomings and drawbacks

In the context of an organisation seeking continuous improvement, BS 5750 has a number of shortcomings and drawbacks. This is not implied criticism of the standard: it was not designed for this purpose. We see the main drawbacks as:

- *The role of the manager:* the word leadership does not appear in BS 5750. Standards are concerned with procedures and manuals. They do not seek to improve the way that people work with each other, or ensure that the process of management allows people to take pride in their work, to be able to achieve job satisfaction or achieve self-esteem. In particular it does not consider the role and behaviour of managers in improving processes and in supporting, empowering and coaching their people. It is therefore of little benefit in creating a culture in which continuous improvement will thrive.

- *Culture:* we refer many times to fear and its effect in inhibiting the commitment and contribution of people. BS 5750 has nothing to say about people afraid to speak out about quality problems, afraid to ask questions, unwilling to ask for training or direction, afraid to report defective or worn out equipment and, most importantly, afraid to suggest ways of improving.
- *The customer:* BS 5750 concentrates on defining processes and procedures that ensure specifications are met. It assumes that the specification truly reflects what customers actually want, whereas in reality the customer knows or cares little about his supplier's internal technical specification.
- *Continuous improvement*: there is no emphasis on prevention of mistakes. On the contrary, guidance is provided as to how to use the existing management system to deal with them. Nor does it mention analysis of causes of problems or mention the need to examine how future mistakes could be avoided. It does not advise eliminating anything, not even bad working habits and practices. Although the standard does refer to the desirability of encouraging the development of new processes and innovation, we conclude that this is incidental to BS 5750 but fundamental to Total Quality.
- *Efficiency:* the emphasis in BS 5750 is on documenting procedures. If existing procedures are inefficient, there is a risk of merely formalising that inefficiency. However, some organisations have reported that the process of documenting and standardising existing procedures has identified inefficiencies which they have been able to remove.
- *Involvement:* registration is usually achieved by a small internal team. It does not involve greatly the people who work in the processes being documented, and they may remain untouched and unaffected by registration.
- *Effort*: BS 5750 usually demands much effort, depending on the extent to which process documentation already exists. The amount of effort over a typical timescale of 6 to 12 months or more demands that organisations be convinced that BS 5750 will generate commensurate benefits for them. Another risk is that after all the effort, the temptation for management to sit back and bask in the reflected glory of their registration certificate is very strong.

Criteria for determining whether to apply for registration

In considering whether to register, organisations should consider the following:

- *Customers:* BS 5750 provides evidence of a degree of commitment to quality. In some industry sectors where BS 5750 has been a minimum requirement for suppliers for some time, customers are now insisting on a commitment to Total Quality as well, and actively working with their suppliers to help them improve their quality.
- *Competitors:* if the trend is towards registration – even without customer insistence – it may be that a company cannot afford to be left behind in what might suddenly establish itself as a competitive standard.
- *Benefits:* where an organisation already has clearly documented policies and procedures the scope for benefits through registration are limited.
- *Alternatives:* organisations need to consider whether their objectives could be better served by alternative approaches to quality improvement, such as Total Quality. Another alternative for some organisations may be a customer 'charter'.

Summary

BS 5750 is a systems, records and documentation approach that has been very effective for some companies. By focusing on the procedures for producing required standards of quality, it provides a platform on which a process of continuous improvement can subsequently be built. It is not incompatible with Total Quality: it can be a very good starting point. But it is simply not enough.

Further reading

There are a great many publications on the subject of Total Quality. The following provide a useful starting point, and most provide further references. Of all the books produced by the gurus, Deming's is essential reading:

- Dr W. Edwards Deming, *Out of the Crisis*, Massachusetts Institute of Technology, Center for Advanced Engineering Study, 1986; Cambridge University Press, 1988.

There are also several writers who are associated with Deming, of which the following are useful and readable:

- William W. Sherkenbach, *Deming's Road to Continual Improvement*, SPC Press, 1991.
- Mary Walton, *The Deming Management Method*, Dodd, Mead & Co, 1986; Mercury Books, 1989.
- Rafael Aguayo, *Dr Deming: The Man who Taught the Japanese about Quality*, Mercury Books, 1991.

In addition, the British Deming Association produces a great deal of material, in the form of booklets, conference proceedings and related publications. They can be contacted at the following address:

British Deming Association
2 Castle Street
Salisbury
Wiltshire
SP1 1BB

Telephone: 0722 412138

The following are by eminent Japanese writers:

- Masaaki Imai, *Kaizen*, McGraw-Hill, 1986.
- Kaoru Ishikawa, *What Is Total Quality Control? The Japanese Way*, Prentice-Hall, 1985.

Juran and Crosby are two other gurus:

- J. M. Juran, *Juran on Quality by Design*, Macmillan, 1992.
- Philip B. Crosby, *Quality Is Free*, McGraw-Hill, 1979.

The following provide good practical advice:

- Mal Owen, *SPC and Continuous Improvement*, IFS Publications, 1989.
- Peter Scholtes, *The Team Handbook*, Joiner, 1988.

The following are remarkable books that focus particularly on the cultural and behavioural aspects of Total Quality. *Zapp!* is written as a fable: do not be put off. IBM is reputed to have 25,000 copies of it for internal management training.

- William C. Byham with Jeff Cox, *Zapp!*, Business Books Ltd, 1991.
- John Seddon, *I Want You to Cheat! The Unreasonable Guide to Service and Quality in Organisations*, Vanguard Press, 1992.